MANGO CULTIVATION AND MARKETING IN INDIA

Prof. Gangadhar Banerjee
M.A. (Eco.), Ph.D. (Eco.), LLB, Pragya (Hindi)

Sri Srijeet Banerji
M.Sc. (Comp. Science) and M.S.
(Cyber Law and Information Security)

ABHIJEET PUBLICATIONS

NEW DELHI 110002

ABHIJEET PUBLICATIONS
4658-A, 1st Floor, Ambika Bhawan
21 Ansari Road, Daryaganj
New Delhi 110002
Phone: 011-2325944, 65698474
E-mail: abhijeetpublication@gmail.com

MANGO CULTIVATION AND MARKETING IN INDIA

First Published 2012

ISBN 978-93-81136-45-4

PRINTED IN INDIA

Published by J.K. Singh for Abhijeet Publications, New Delhi-110002, Lasertypeset by Gaurav Graphics, New Delhi and Printed at Asian Offset, Delhi.

Preface

The treatise on "Mango Cultivation, Processing and Marketing in India—Prospects and Retrospect' is based on "Commodity Specific Study on Mango" undertaken in Andhra Pradesh, Maharashtra and West Bengal. It is a part of the project entrusted to the author by NABARD.

The book contains *12 chapters*. *Chapter 1* deals with "Introduction" which covers botanical name of mango and its cultivation; important characteristics of mango and its nutritional value; India's position of world mango and development of Agri-Export Zone of mango in India. "Objectives and Methodology" has been incorporated in *Chapter 2 that takes* into account selection of states/ districts/ sample size and data collection, data analysis. Besides, attempt has been endeavoured to work out capital/ expenses/ gross profit ratios, break- even- point, net present worth, benefit cost ratio, internal rate of return, marketing efficiency, and export competitiveness. *Chapter 3* incorporates "India's Place in the World Mango". In the process area, production and productivity of mango to total fruit crops; area, production and productivity of mango in major producing countries of the world; and area, production, yield of mango—World and India have been analyzed. In *Chapter 4* the book has made "Trend

Analysis "in respect of area, production and yield of mango between India and selected States. *Chapter 5* of the book concentrates on "Profile of Mango Growers and Mango Orchards". Further, age-wise, level education wise, social group wise, occupational pattern wise and family size wise distribution of mango growers have been dwelt upon. Similarly distribution of mango orchards by acreage, and age etc have find place in the book. The book has outlined in details of "Cultivation and Cultural Practices" of mango in *Chapter 6* which covers land preparation, sapling pattern, post planting nursing, application of fertilizer, diseases and pest attack, inter crop, cultural schedules; irregular bearing habit of mango tree, recommended practices, and harvesting.

Marketing is the major issue in all agriculture and horticulture crops. Thus, proper weightage has been given to examine the "Marketing Aspects of Mango: Role of Different Channels, Value Chain, Market Arrivals and Price Spread" in *Chapter 7. Here attempt has been confined to* analyze the role of different channels; market arrivals and price spread; marketing channels of mango, pre-harvest contractors, UP country traders, mango processing units, village Traders and commission agents. Roles of UP country traders/commission agents/transport operators in price fixation of all Alphanso and Kesar mangos in Maharashtra have been examined. Efficiency of marketing channels; marketing cost and average price realized, marketing expenses and their share in price of one kg of Alphanso Mango and relationship between price and arrivals of m have been calculated. *Chapters 8 and 9* dovetail "Economics of Mango orchards and Mango Processing" which has been divided in two sections. Section I brings out various aspects of raw mango products like pickles, amchoor, mango slices, green mango beverages; and ripe mango products which includes pulp, mango jelly, beverage, squash, mango leather etc. Besides, different processing activities in mango chain; manufacturing process of mango pulps have been penned. Investment cost of pulp mango, cost and returns of processing mango into canned pulps, various profitability ratios have been estimated. Mango jelly cluster which incorporates manufacturing of mango jelly, and economics of jelly making have been attempted. Section 11 makes an over view of mango processing Units in Chittor, of Andhra Pradesh, status of processed mango in Chittor, forward and backward linkages of mango processing industry, economic feasibility of mango processing plants, employment details, cost, returns and profitability, feasibility of mango processing units, internal rate of return and pay back-period. *Chapter 10* outlines "Post-harvest Management of Mangoes, Exports of Mango Based Products and Performance of Excise Zone ". While dealing with this chapter, efforts have been exercised on aspects relating to grading, desapping, and processing; post-harvest operation, pack house; grading and packing centre; (sorting, cleaning and washing, fungicide treatment, size, grading and waxing, packing) pre cooling; cold storage-and transportation. Export Performance of mango (fresh Mango, mango pulp and other mango based products); export prices of mango and mango pulp have been evaluated. *Chapter 11* contains "Supply Chain Management and Credit Support". It covers Agri Export Zone, Growers / Processors' Federation, input supply; credit support, repayment performance of bank loan, credit availability. "Constraints, Issues, Strategies and Policy Suggestions"have been outlined in *chapter 12*. The major constraints faced by the mango growers are inadequate extension services, infrastructural bottlenecks, lack of export promotion, international competition, absence of uniformity of Shape / size / Colour. To enhance exports, development / strengthening of post harvest infrastructure, establishment of pack Houses/Cold Storage/Vapour Heat Treatment, good net working of rail and road transport; existence of processing /marketing facilities, availment of institutional credit.

The book made some policy prescription like (i) attainment of growth and sustainability, (ii) strengthening of forward and backward linkages, (iii) launching of contract farming, (iv) ensuring promotion of domestic consumption, (v) formation of Cooperative Societies, (vi) availability of adequate quality planting materials,(vii) promotion of Mango as Horticulture Crops, (viii) uprooting the senile and unproductive orchards, (ix) transferring the latest technology to marginal and small farmers, (x) setting of pack-houses with washing, waxing, packing, pre-cooling and storage including Refrigerated Vans for Transport,(xi) establishment of Vapour Heat Treatment Plant, (xii) availability of more institutional credit, (xiii) streamlining data on credit flow to mango and (xiv) formation of Self-help Groups

The author is indebted to Dr K.G.Karmarkar, Director (Operation and Research), SPJAIN, Institute of Management Studies and Research, Mumbai, and Former Managing Director, NABARD, who was kind enough to provide valuable suggestions for improvement of the manuscript. We are really indebted to him. Further, we are thankful to Dr A.K.Bandyopadhyay, necessary guidance, constant inspiration and encouragement throughout. I must place on record my heartfelt thanks to Shri L.M.Palke for his valuable suggestions.

I shall be failing my duty if I do not acknowledge the authors Shri K.C. Badatya/ R.H.V. Ratnababu, Assistant General Managers; B.Maghi, Assistant General Manager, S.R.Das/ Smt Aswari Amelkar, Assistant Manager and Subhash Seaphim / Nivedita Pal, Assistant General Manager / Manager for their report. I express my sincere thanks to Anupam Pattanaik, Assistant Manager, NABCONS for his help in many ways.

The Authors

Contents

Contents

1

Introduction

1.1 Botanical Name of Mango and its Cultivation

The Mango, *Mangifera indigo L.*, belongs to the family of *Anacardiaceae*, is one of the most important tropical and subtropical fruits of the world and is popular both in fresh and processed forms. It is called king of fruits on account of its nutritive value, taste, attractive fragnence and health promoting qualities. In many languages it is called the mother of all tropical fruits and is the national fruit of India. Mango has been in cultivation in Indian subcontinent for well over 4,000 years and has been the most favorite fruit since ages. Historical facts revealed that mango was introduced to India archipelago from the main land. Some researchers are of the view that it had originated in the Indo–Burma region. Presently, besides India, it is being cultivated world over especially, in the South and South-East Asian countries, African countries, tropical Australia and the USA. In USA mango is grown mostly in Florida, and Hawai. Mango is also grown in Venezuela, Mexico, Brazil, Carribbean Islands and Cambodia.

1.2 Mango in Sanskrit Scriptures

Mango has been portrayed in the ancient paintings and sculptures, Hindu folklore and mythology, legends and in the sacred Sanskrit Scriptures dating back to 2000 BC. Mango continued to be grown as a seedling tree until the establishment of the Moghul rule in India. During the Moghul period seedling trees were designated as distinct varieties and attempts were made to propagate them vegetative. Akbar, the great Moghul emperor, (1556 to 1605 AD), planted mango orchards of 0.1 million trees near Darbhanga in Bihar. This was the time when Mango actually got the royal patronage. In India the first systematic record of varieties of mango was available in "Ain-e-Akabari", the biography of Akbar, AD 1590, by Abu Fazal. However, mango orchard remained the prerogative of the "Rajas and Nawabs" for a very long time. Mango cultivation has now been taken up commercially.

1.3 Important Characteristics of Mango

The mango tree is a large branched perennial tree with height of 30-40 m and a crown radius spreading about 10 m. The flowers are produced in terminal panicles of 10-40 cm long and each flower has 5 petals of 5-10 mm long. After flowering, the fruit, which is a drupe, takes three to six months to ripe. The Mango fruit varies considerably in size, shape, color, presence of fiber, flavor, taste and several other characters. The shape of the fruit varies from rounded to ovate-oblong or longish, with the length ranging from 2.5 to 30 cm in different varieties. The weight of mango goes up to 2.5 kg for some varieties. However, the average size of mango available to India marked weighs about 200-350 grams. The ripe fruit is yellow, orange and red in colour; usually reddish on the side facing the sun. Mango is well adapted to tropical and sub tropical climates. The ideal temperature ranged for mango is 24^0 to 30^0 C during the growing season, along with high humidity. A rainfall ranging from 890 mm to 1,015 mm in a year is considered to be ideal for growing mangoes. Dry weather before blossoming is conducive to profuse flowering. Mangoes, ripe or unripe, are widely used as a fresh fruit. It is also used to make juice, milk shake, pulp, jam, jelly, pickle, and chutni. Ripe mango is often cut into thin layers, desiccated, folded and then cut and sold as mango chewy bras. Pieces of the fruit can be mashed and used in ice-cream. Dried unripe mango, mainly amchur is used as a spice in India.

1.4 Nutritional Value of Mango

Mango is nutritious and excellent source of carotene as compared to other fruits. The nutritive value per 100 gram mango is presented in *Annexure 1.*

A 100 gram of edible portion of the mango contains about 1990 μg of beta-carotene (vitamin A), which is much higher than in other fruits. The total carotenoides in mango increase with the stage of ripening. Eating mangoes in the season may provide a store of vitamin A in the liver, sufficient to last for the rest of the year and highly beneficial for the prevention of vitamin A deficient disorder, like night blindness. Mangoes, both ripe and unripe, are very good a source of vitamin C. About 16 mg of vitamin C is present in 100 gram of mango. Ripe mango provides a good source of calories and supplies 74 kcal per 100 gram.

1.5 India's Position in World of Mango

India ranks first among World's mango producing countries accounting for 52.6 per cent of world's mango production. It is grown over an area of 1.2 million hectares in the country producing 11.0 million tones. It constitutes

22.1 per cent of total area under fruit crops (5.6 million hectares) and 22.9 per cent of total production of fruits (47.9 million tons) in the country. Uttar Pradesh, Gujarat, Andhra Pradesh, Maharashtra, Bihar, Karnataka, Tamil Nadu, and Punjab are major mango producing states. The mangoes contribute a major share in the exports of horticulture item as well. During 2008-09, the country's exports of mango and mango-based products were reported at Rs 627.81 crore.

1.6 Commercialization in Agriculture—Traditional to New crops

Mechanization, diversification and commercialization in agriculture resulted in shifting of cropping pattern from traditional crops to new crops, which had contributed to the increased area and production under Mango. Changing demand pattern also contributed significantly to shifting of more area and production of mango. However, marketing and processing of mango have not picked up commensurate with the level of production. Further, supportive mechanism in the form of agriculture inputs, post-harvest infrastructure set up, such as packaging, pre-cooling, cold storage, pack houses, marketing system, and institutional credit have not come up in proportionate to the increase in production of fruit.

Even though India is the world's largest producer of mango, it accounts for less than one per cent of global mango trade. Around 95 per cent of India's mango exports are routed to the Middle-East countries, whereas only 5 per cent is channeled to other countries like Europe, America, Japan, Hongkong etc. Further, exports of mangoes in the processed form remain limited. Besides, high perishability, seasonality in production and absence of post-harvest facility, lack of standardized supply chain system, etc. resulted in loss of about 25-30 per cent of the total mango production during post-harvest period.

This reduces further availability of fruits for consumption, value addition and export. There are issues such as weak institutional arrangements, limited marketing facilities, lack of coordination among the various organizations etc. have acted as hindrance in the growth of mango. The whole lot of the issues encompasses the supply chain system (SCS) within the mango processing sector. The importance of this study on mango lies in addressing these issues affecting the above mentioned parameters.

1.7 Development under Agri-Export Zone (AEZ) of Mango in India

The Government of India in the year 2001-02 has announced formation of AEZs in selected areas of different states and later it was incorporated in the Export Import (EXIM) Policy. The concept of Agri Export Zone attempts to take a comprehensive look at a particular produce/ product located in a contiguous area for the purpose of developing and sourcing the raw materials, their processing / packing, leading to final exports. The entire report is centered on a cluster approach of identifying the potential products, the geographical region in which these are grown and adopting an end to end approach of integrating the entire process right from the stage of production till it reaches the market. In India 11 Mango AEZ's were formed in various regions, the details are given in *Annexure* 2.

Out of 11 mango AEZs in India, 5 AEZs are located in Andhra Pradesh followed by Maharashtra (2), and I each in Uttar Pradesh, Gujarat, Tamil Nadu and West Bengal. In Andhra Pradesh there are 10 districts where mangoes are cultivated while these are 9 districts in Maharashtra, 7 districts in Uttar Pradesh, 8 in Gujarat, 2 in West Bengal and 5 in Tamil Nadu. The State Agricultural Marketing Board is the nodal agency for implementation of the AEZs. The National Horticulture Mission (NHM) identified mango as one of the core commodities having scope for further growth. The Agricultural and Processed Food Products Export Development Authority (APEDA) since its inception in 1986, has been playing a major role in the export of mango and mango based products by providing various services at both national and international level.

1.8 Rationale of the Study

Added to these the selected states enjoy a favourable environment, which inter-alia include suitable agro climatic conditions, huge domestic market, cheap labor etc. All these offer a tremendous potential to increase the overall production of mango and mango based products, thus contributing to the nation's exportable surplus on the other. Against this back drop a commodity specific study on mango was planned in the states of Andhra Pradesh, Maharashtra and West Bengal in order to have a full perspective of the commodity in its varied facets, i.e. production, processing, marketing, exports, cost of cultivation etc..The present report is the consolidation of three state reports.

1.9 Organization of the Study Report

The report has been organized in **twelve** Chapters. Chapter **one** covers introduction and Chapter two outlines the objectives, methodology and sample design. Chapter three devotes India's place in world mango. Chapters four and five analyze the trends of area, production and yield of mango in India and selected states as well as profile of mango growers/orchards respectively. Chapter six dwells upon cultivation and cultural practices of mango, while chapter seven describes marketing aspects focusing on role played by different channels, value chains, market arrivals and price spread etc in select states. The economics of mango orchards and processing have been worked out in Chapter eight and nine respectively. Chapter ten assesses post-harvest management, exports of mango based products and performance of excise zone; and chapter eleven describes supply chain management, and credit support. Constraints and strategies for furthering production, processing and export of mango have been presented in Chapter twelve.

1.10 The Scope of the Study

The findings and recommendations of the study are based on sample of mango growers, mango processors, traders, exporters, mango growers' association etc. in all the three states i.e., Andhra Pradesh, Maharashtra and West Bengal. Besides, it is dependent on discussions with district level functionaries like, officials from the Department of Horticulture (DOH) at the district level, marketing committees, banks, District Development Managers (DDMs), Lead Development Managers (LDMs) of the study districts as also the final consumers of mango and mango based products. Generally, mango arrivals and prices vary considerably across different markets even within a given district. Consequently price spread, market efficiency and other related parameters differ. Therefore, the findings of the study presented in this report should be interpreted judiciously and should not be generalized across the state and districts.

2

Objectives, Methodology and Sample Design

This chapter is confined to objectives, study design and methodology. The specific objectives of the Study are as follows:—

2.1 Objectives

To analyze the growth patterns in area, production and productivity of mango in selected states vis-à-vis India.

To study the cultivation practices of mango as also the adoption of modern technology, along with calculating the economics of mango orchards and processing.

To describe the aspects relating to marketing of mango and mango based products, price spread, various channels, their efficiency etc.

To describe Process involved in mango processing, its economics and issues affecting the processing industry etc.

To ascertain the export performance of mango and mango based products, role of AEZs in export promotion etc.

To analyze the post-harvest management practices of mango as also availability of infrastructure and backward and forward linkages for and effective supply chain system for mango and mango related products.

To identify the constraints of mango cultivation and suggest remedial measures.

2.2 Methodology and Sample Design

While addressing the issues affecting mango as a horticultural commodity, the study adopted 'FARM to PLATE' (FTP) approach. The study concentrated on issues involved from production of mango to its marketing and consumption by the households. In production stage, the study dealt with the 'Farm Economics' to understand the cost of cultivation and income accrued to the cultivators of mango. In the processing stage the study attempted to analyze different products of value addition and economics of such value addition. Lastly, in marketing stage, the study focused on identification of different channels of marketing, price spread, marketing efficiency etc. and identified critical issues involved for improving efficiency. The study also outlined 'Supply Chain Management System' (SCMS) covering the collaboration and harmonized relationship covering input supply, production, harvesting, marketing, storage, processing etc.

2.3 Selection of States

A comprehensive view on the criteria of production and area was taken to select 3 states viz., Andhra Pradesh, Maharashtra and West Bengal for the present study. Taking into account the last five years data (2005-06 to 2008-09) on area, India, on an average covers an area of 2,070 thousand hectares under mango cultivation. The share of Maharashtra was highest at 22.1 per cent, followed by

Andhra Pradesh (20%), while it was lowest for West Bengal (3.5%). In terms of production, Andhra Pradesh contributes 27 per cent, Maharashtra 5.5 per cent and West Bengal 4 per cent of All India production.

2.4 Selection of Districts

In Andhra Pradesh production of mango is concentrated in all the districts. However, in terms of ranking, Krishna district in Coastal Region (4.96 lakh MT), Chittoor district in Rayalseema Region (3.91 lakh MT) and Khammam district in Telengana Region (3.34 lakh MT) stand first, second and third position respectively. Further, a number of mango processing units (pulp and jelly making) are located in Chittoor and Krishna districts. With a view to harnessing the export potential of mangoes produced in the state, AEZs for mango pulp in Chittoor district and AEZ for fresh mango for Krishna district has been set up in the state. Accordingly, Krishna and Chittoor districts were selected for the study. Mango jelly making units were confined to East Godavari district and a few jelly making units were visited for the purpose of the study. Accordingly, East Godavari district was also selected. From both the districts, four blocks were selected in Chittor district and five blocks in Krishna district considering the area, production and arrival of mango to the nearest market yard. Damancheruvu, Chittoor, Triputi and Bangarupalem blocks were considered from Chittoor district and Nuzivid, Tiruvur, Agiripalli, Vissannapet and Gampalagudum blocks were taken into account in Krishna district.

In Maharashtra Alphonso and Kesar varieties of mango are of immense economic importance to the rural people of the state. The major Alphonso growing districts are Ratnagiri, Raigad, Thane, and Sindhudurg. The Kesar variety is grown in Aurangabad, Jalna, Beed, Latur, Ahmedanagar and Nasik districts. It was, therefore, decided to take up both the varieties of mango (i.e Alphonso and Kesar) and conduct a study in two major districts growing these two varieties. Accordingly, Sindhudurg district was selected for Alphonso mango. The Aurangabad district was selected for the study of Kesar mango. In each districts at least two blocks were covered. Jalna district, adjoining Aurangabad was also covered to study the Kesar variety of mango.

In West Bengal, Malda and Murshidabad districts in 2005 covered an area of 25,250 hectare and 11,564 hectare respectively under mango cultivation. These two districts together constituted 53 per cent of total area of mango in the state. Therefore Malda and Murshidabad districts were selected in West Bengal.

2.5 Sample Size of Selected States

A total of 186 samples were selected from three states. Of which Andhra Pradesh had 75 samples representing 40.33 per cent of total followed by Maharashtra 59 accounting for 31.72 per cent and West Bengal 52 constituting 27.95 per cent. State-wise sample size is given in table below:-

Table 2.1: Sample Size according to State

Name of the State	*Number of districts*	*Number of sample*	*Share (%)*
Andhra Pradesh	3 (Chittoor,@ Krishna,# East Godavari^)	75	40.33
Maharashtra	2 (Sindhudurg, Aurangabad)	59	31.72
West Bengal	2 (Malda and Murshidabad)	52	27.95
Total	7	**186**	**100**

Source: Field investigation.

@ Chittoor—36, # Krishna—33 and East Godavari—6

Again total samples were distributed by various categories which are presented below:-

Table 2.2: Distribution of Samples by Category

Category of sample/State	*Andhra Pradesh*	*Mahara-shtra*	*West Bengal*	*Total*	*Share*
Mango Growers	42	40	10	92	49.47
Mango Processors	18	03	12	33	17.75
Traders /Exporters	15	04	10	29	15.59
Banks	-	07	-	07	3.76
Nursery Owners	-	-	10	10	5.37
Others	-	5*	10@	15	8.06
Total	**75**	**59**	**52**	**186**	**100.00**

Source—Field investigation.

* Mango growers Associations/ Cooperative (2), Marketing Mandi (1), Farmers Club, (1) Transport Agent (1), and @ Contractor.

Mango growers constituted 49.47 per cent of total sample while Mango processors and Traders/Exporters represented 17.75 per cent and 15.59 per cent of total respectively. Share of total samples to other "others" were only 8.06 per cent (Table 2.2).

2.6 Data Collection

The study is based on both primary and secondary data. **Secondary data** was collected mainly from published sources of states and Central government. Publications from Agricultural and Processed Food Products Export Development Authority (APEDA), National Horticulture Board (NHB), Department of Marketing and Directorate of Economics and Statistics (DoES), State Governments, Websites of different organizations and institutions were made use of. Information was also obtained from nurseries, Farmers Clubs, Mandis, Mango Growers Associations, transport agents. Statistics were gathered from other input suppliers, units involved in post harvest handling of mango, district level nodal officers AEZs, market yards, banks and financial institutions etc.

Primary data was collected through direct interview method using pre designed schedules/structured questionnaires. The actual investment cost for establishment of the orchard was collated items-wise from the sample farmers. Such items include land preparation, pitch digging, blasting cost of plant, propping, compost, fertilizers, chemicals, irrigation, fencing around the orchard, watch and ward etc. The expenses incurred during the initial five years of plantation were taken in the investment cost. Annual maintenance cost included all the cultivation expenses (paid out cost + imputed value of inputs, including family labor). Availability of planting materials and other inputs was ascertained from progressive farmers, nurseries, inputs agents, research centers and government departments. The package of farming practices was also confirmed from the research centers and Agriculture departments as also infrastructure for post harvest management of mango. The data on prevailing practices, constraints and the scope for processing of mango were ascertained from a few food processing units. The marketing cost data covering plucking, packaging, transport to the market, market fee etc..were obtained from farmers. These details were also got and crossed checked with the information gathered from the transport operators and commission agents. The data on price realized was obtained from the farmers and got it cross cheeked with the data from the marketing committee for the year 2005-06. The process of bidding in the market was ascertained from Agricultural Produce Marketing Committees (APMCs). The information in this regard, furnished by the sample farmers and growers' associations were also appraised. Some of the whole sellers/commission agents purchased good quality mangoes for exports directly from farmers while a few of them were engaged in graded mangoes for exports by purchasing the same from in the local markets. Such exporters were interviewed for ascertaining various costs, formalities, quality norms and prices realized by them. The requirement of bank credit for mango cultivation and its availability were ascertained from bank branches and controller of some banks. The views of District Development Manager (DDMs), NABARD and the Lead District Manager (LDM) of the respective districts on credit related matters were also considered.

2.7 Data Analysis

Various tools of analysis, in addition to tabular forms, percentages etc, were used to assess the feasibility of the mango units are:-

1. *Capital Ratio*
   (a) Capital turnover ratio = Gross income\Average capital investment
   (b) Capital per unit of gross income = Total capital invested on the mango unit\gross income from the unit
2. *Expense Income Ratio*
   (a) Operating ratio= Total operating expenses/gross Income
   (b) Fixed ratio= Fixed Expenses/Gross Income
   (c) Gross Profit Ratio = Gross income/Gross Expenses
3. *Project Evaluation Techniques*
   (a) Net Present Worth (NPW) = Sum total of discounted benefit - Sum total of discounted costs
   (b) Benefit Cost Ratio = Sum total of discounted benefit/ Sum total of discounted costs

(c) Internal Rate of Return = Lower discount rate+ difference between the two discount rates x{NPW of benefit at lower discount rate/NPW of benefit at higher discount rate, sign ignored]

(d) Break Even Point=Fixed Cost/Sale price per unit-Variable cost per unit = F/(P-V)

4. *Marketing Efficiency (ME)*

The Marketing efficiency is arrived through the concept of 'price spread'. The price spread is defined as the difference between the price per unit of output paid by the consumer and that received by the producer. This difference is accounted for by various costs, particularly marketing costs, incurred by the market intermediaries and the margins retained by them. In the absence of direct linkage between the mango grower and the consumer, it is the middle man who has been taking advantage of the situation. And indicator of the efficiency of any supply chain is the extent of the price spread between the producers and the consumer. A higher price spread would indicate a lower efficiency. The producer's share in the consumer price is high then the marketing efficiency is high. The formula used to arrive at the market efficiency is as mentioned below—

$Ps = Pf / Pc \times 100$,

Where Ps = Producer's share in consumer's price, Pf= Price of the Produce received by the farmers and Pc = Price paid by the consumer. In other words, ME= Summation of Intermediary Margins/(Consumer Price-Producers' Farm Gate Price.

5. *Export Competitiveness (EC)*

Export competitiveness of mango is measured by Nominal Protection Coefficient (NPC). The NPC is the ratio of domestic price to FOB price/ border price/reference price of commodity.

NPC = Pd/Pfob

Where, NPC= Nominal Protection Coefficient

Pd= Domestic Price

Pfob= Price fixed at the time of consignment for export (Freight on Board)

Domestic price is the wholesale price in the post harvest season. FOB price has been provided by the exporters and this has been calculated by using international price adjusted for freight charges, marketing and packing cozies. If the resulting NPC is less than unity commodity is treated as globally more competitive.

2.8 The Reference Year of the Study was 2005-06.

i.e, 700. The small firms on the other hands employ only 256 workers. However, most of the employment is on a part time basis, processing industry being a seasonal industry. The small firms produce 860 tons of mango pulp per unit whereas the large firms produce 5,995 tons. Total revenue generated, on an average, varies from Rs. 161.25 lakh for small firms to Rs. 1361.6 lakh for large firms. Net revenue available for small firms was Rs. 11.25 lakh and Rs. 40.93 lakh for large firms. Thus, it is evident that the processing firms are profitable.

The operating ratio ranges from 0.76 for small firms and 0.82 for large firms. This signifies that every rupee of gross income a substantial portion of operation cost is incurred. The fixed ratio varies from 0.13 for medium firms to 0.17 for small firms. The gross ratio is less than one signifying the efficient operation of firms. However, it is substantially high and varies from 0.93 for small firms to 0.97 for large firms. This reveals that a large portion of gross income is utilized for meeting the total expenses. It also reveals that small firms are more efficient than other size class of firms.

The capital turnover ratio ranges from 0.81 for small firms to 0.91 for large firms revealing that every rupee investment by small firms generates gross income of 81 paisa. This measures show that large firms are more efficient than the small firms.The rate of return on investment gives a better picture of efficiency. The value of rate of return on investment varies from 0.027 for large firms to 0.056 for small firms revealing that every rupee of capital investment generates a net return of 3 paisa and 6 paisa. This measure shows that small firms are more efficient than large firms.

The IRR of small firms (19.31%) is the highest followed by that of large firms (17.5%) and medium firms (13.87%). All three size class of firms is available as their internal rate of return (IRR) is greater than the opportunity cost of capital. Thus, the small firms rank the highest and the medium firms rank the lowest as per the IRR criteria. The payback period explains the number of years in which the investment is paid back by the project. It is observed that investment in mango processing plant has least payback period for small firms (5.25 years) followed by that of large firms (5.99 years) and medium firms (6.89 years). The shorter payback period for mango processing plants provides an important opportunity for an entrepreneur.

The breakeven point for small firms (Rs. 113.54 lakh) is the lowest followed by medium firms (Rs. 380.97 lakh) and the large firms (Rs. 1138.85 lakh) respectively. The BEP in physical terms for small firms with 605.52 tons is the least followed by medium and large firms with production of 1746.82 tons and 5014.25 tons respectively. It is implied that firm should operate at a level generating gross revenue and producing output above these values by the respective firm size classes to be profitable.

Export of fresh mango from Krishna district has always been below 500 MT per annum. Although there are mango growers' cooperative organizations, they have not been able to plan an organized production and marketing system. They have also not been able to reduce the marketing channels. To smoothen out the supply chain management (SCM) for mango processing sector, 'Chittor District Canners' Federation was formed during 1991. Later it was rechristened as Chittor District Fruit Processors Federation.

Another important input in the pulp industry is the packaging and packing material, such as cans, aseptic bag, and cartons. The units undertaking the processing on job work basis are supplied with require can material, labels, and packing materials by Export Houses which have provided production orders.

3

India's Place in the World of Mango

This chapter deals with India's share in world of mango in terms of area, production, yield and export. In the process the chapter outlines the major mango producing countries and their share in total area and production of world mango.

3.1 Global Scenario

India's Position of Mango Production in Fruits and Vegetables in World Market

According to Food and Agriculture Organization (FAO) Mango is one of the six major fruits crops in the world. India's position of mango in production of various fruits and vegetables in international ranking is presented below:

Table 3.1: India's Position in Production of Fruits and Vegetables in World

Crop	*Rank*	*Crop*	*Rank*
Apple	10	Brinjal	2
Banana	1	Cabbage	2
Mango	1	Cauliflower	1
Papaya	2	Peas	1

Pine Apple	4	Onion	2
Grapes	10	Potato	3
Cashew	1	Total Vegetables	2
Coconut	3		
Total Fruits	2		

Source: Indian Horticulture Data Base, 2009.

It is evident from the data presented in the above Table 3.1 that India's mango ranks first in the international market.

3.2 Area, Production, and Productivity of Mango to Total Fruit Crops

Mango accounts for more than one third (37.8%) of total area under fruit crops and about 20 per cent of total fruit production in 2008-09. This is evident from the Table 3.2:—

Table 3.2: Area, Production and Yield of Mango to Total Fruit Crops

Year	*Area (in thousand hectare)*	*Percentage to total area under fruit crops(%)*	*Production (in thousand MT)*	*Percentage to total fruit production (%)*	*Yield (in kg/ hectare)*
1991-92	1077.6	37.5	8715.6	30.4	8.100
2001-02	1575.8	39.3	10020.2	23.3	6.400
2005-06	2080.7	39.1	12663.1	22.9	6100
2008-09	2309.0	37.8	12750.0	18.6	5500
CAGR	**7.62**	**-**	**3.08**	**-**	**-3.15**

Source: Indian Horticulture Data Base 2009, CAGR= Compounded Annual Growth Rate.

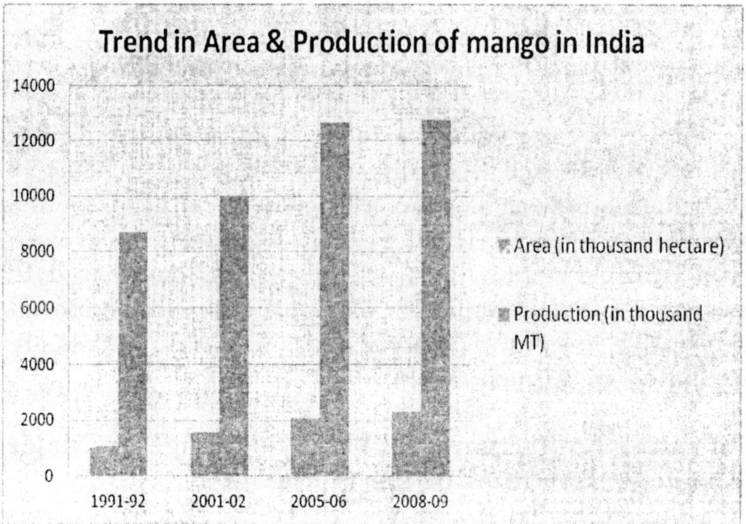

Graphic 3.1: Trends in Area and Production of Mango

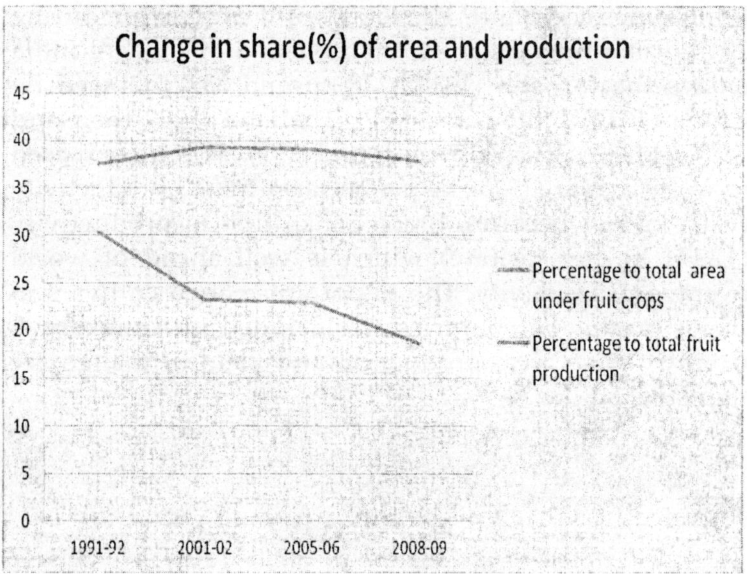

Graphic 3.2 Shares of Area and Production of Mango to Total Fruit Crops

Share of India's area under mango to total fruits area in 1987-88 was 43.5 per cent which declined to 37.8 in 2008-09. Share of mango to total fruit area varied 28.5 to 42.9 per cent. The share of mango to total fruit production started declining over the years. In 1987-88 the share stood at 37.4 per cent which reduced to 18.6 per cent in 2008-09. The CAGR showed that area growth was 7.62 per cent which was quite high compared to growth in production (3.08 %). Productivity experienced a negative growth of 3.15 per cent. Year wise details are exhibited in **Annexure 3.**

3.3 Area, Production and Yield of Mango in Major Producing Countries of the World

Mango is commercially grown in about 83 countries in the world. Major mango producing countries are China, Mexico, Pakistan, Indonesia, Thailand, Nigeria, Brazil, Philippines and Haiti. The total world production during 2010 was estimated at 34,750 thousand MT where India enjoys the top slot (1312.22 thousand MT followed by China (4657.42 thousand MT), Thailand (2222 thousand MT), Mexico (1925.15 thousand MT). When compared to world average (7202 kg per hectare), India's productivity (7065 kg per hectare). Brazil ranks first in productivity (12394 kg per hectare) which is well ahead of world average productivity. The important mango cultivars in major producing countries are included in **Annexure 4**. Country wise area, production and yield of mango are depicted below:

Table 3.3: Area, Production and Yield of Mango in Major producing Countries in 2010@

Name of the country	*Area in (thousand ha.)*	*Share(%) to total*	*Production in (thousand MT)*	*Share(%) to total*	*Yield (Kg./ha.)*
Brazil	89.72	1.86	1112.00	3.20	12394
China	592.89	12.35	4657.42	13.40	7855
Guinea	100.63	2.25	202.15	0.58	1658
India	1860.04	38.55	13056.12	37.76	7065
Indonesia	351.19	7.32	1939.05	5.58	5523
Mexico	211.34	4.38	1925.15	5.54	9123
Nigeria	155.32	3.22	865.28	2.49	5570
Pakistan	185.76	3.85	2015.50	5.80	10850
Philippines	198.79	4.12	1198.86	3.45	6032
Thailand	367.11	7.65	2222.00	6.40	6052
Others	692.21	14.45	5490.50	25.80	7933
Total	**4825.00**	**100.00**	**34750.00**	**100.00**	**7202**

@ Provisional/Estimated, Source: FAO Data Base 2009.

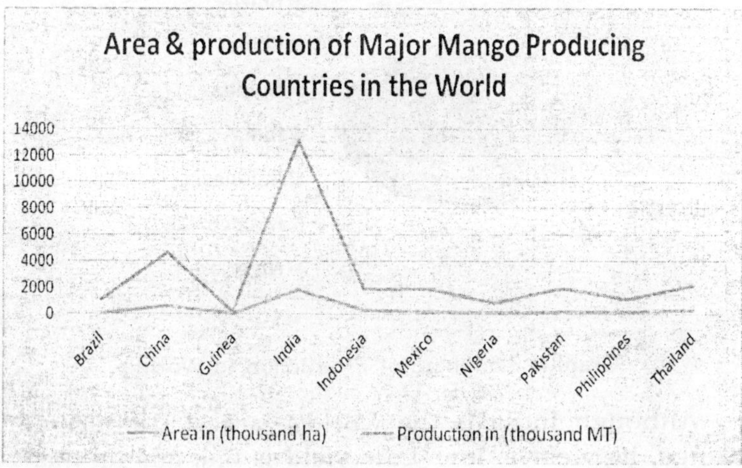

Graphic 3.3: Area and Production of Major Mango Production Countries

Graphic 3.4: Share of Area to World

Graphic 3.5: Share of Production to World

Although India is the world's largest producer of mango, its yield is low. Low yield is one among many problems identified, others being post harvest damage, size of orchards not amenable and absence of procuct brands. Indian mangoes are world famous and have great potential for export as compared to other fruits of the country. The reasons for low productivity of mangoes in India are that most of the commercial cultivars are location specific with long gestation period and alternate bearing habit, viz., Dashehari, Langra, Chausa, Bombay Green, Alphonsa, Banganpalli, Pairi, Himsagar, Kesar, Mulgoa etc.

3.4 Area under Mango—World and India

The world area under mango has been estimated at 4825 thousand hectare whereas India covers an area of 1848 thousand hectares constituting 38.31 per cent of the total area. Details are exhibited below:-

Table 3.4: Area under Mango—World and India

(Area in thousand hectares)

Particulars/ Year	*2004*	*2005*	*2006*	*2007*	*2008*	*2009*	*2010**	*Average*
World	3658	3850	4170	4350	4520	4695	4825	4296
India	1560	1600	1680	1715	1750	1810	1848	1709
Share of India to World (%)	**42.65**	**41.35**	**40.28**	**39.42**	**38.72**	**38.55**	**38.31**	**39.78**

* Estimated, Source: FAO Data Base 2009.

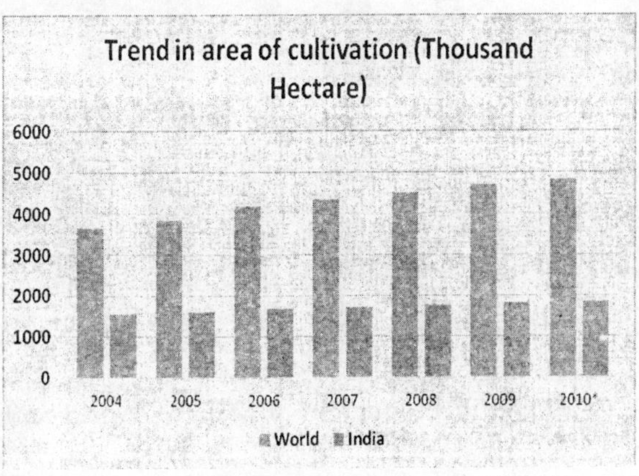

Graphic 3.6: Trends of Area under Mango—World and India

3.5. Trends in Production of Mango—World and India

World production of mango has been estimated at 34750 thousand MT, while India produces 13056 thousand MT representing 37.57 per cent of world production. India's share in world production during 2004-2010 is depicted in Table 3.5:

Table 3.5: Production of Mango—World and India

(Production in thousand metric ton -MT)

Particulars/ Year	*2004*	*2005*	*2006*	*2007*	*2008*	*2009*	*2010**	*Average*
World	25570	27967	29712	31105	33442	33768	34750	30902
India	10873	10800	11752	12014	12294	12752	13056	11934
(%) **	**42.52**	**38.62**	**39.46**	**38.62**	**37.88**	**37.76**	**37.57**	**38.62**

*Estimated, Source: FAO Data Base 2009, ** India's share to World's Production.

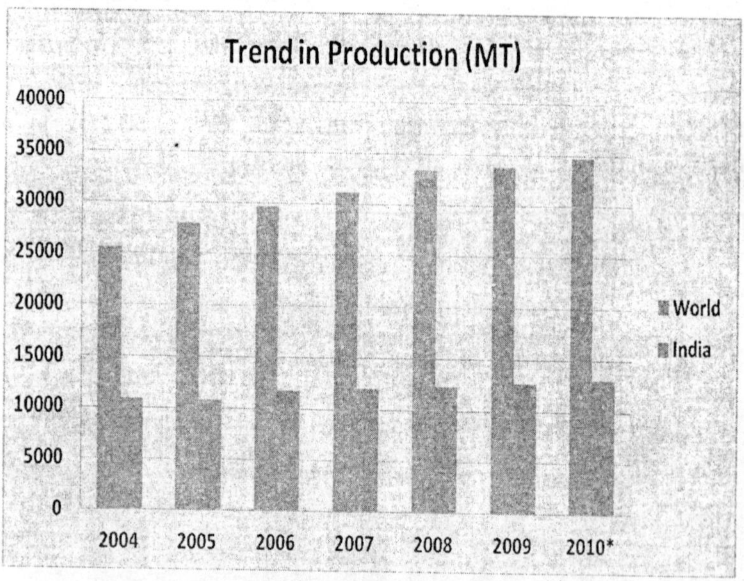

Graphic 3.7: Trends in Production of Mango –World and India

3.6 Yield of Mango—World and India

Yield of mango in the world was 6,990 kg per hectare in 2004, while it was 6,970 kg per hectare in India. Thus, India's yield was lower by 20 kg per hectare compared to world yield during 2004. In 2010 productivity of mango in the world improved by 212 kg per hectare (7,202 kg/ha) and in India by only 95 kg per hectare (7065 kg per hectare). This shows that yield of mango between World and India has slight variation. The position is given in Table 3.6:

Table 3.6: Yield of Mango during 2004-2010—World and India

(Kg per hectare)

Particulars/ Year	*2004*	*2005*	*2006*	*2007*	*2008*	*2009*	*2010**	*Average*
World	6990	7226	7125	7150	7180	7192	7202	7152
India	6970	6750	6995	7005	7025	7045	7065	6979

*Estimated, Source: FAO Data Base 2009.

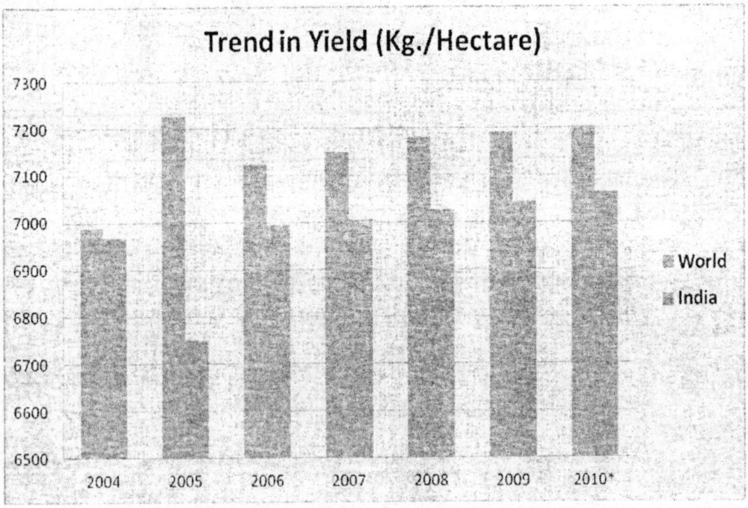

Graphic 3.8: Trends in Yield of Mango—World and India

3.7 Indices of Area, Production and Yield of Mango—World and India

Taking into account 2004 as base year, world production of mango has hiked by 36 per cent in 2010. This was mainly due to enhancement of area by 32 per cent and improvement of yield by 3 per cent. In India, production escalated by 20 per cent during during the period 2004 to 2010. The increase in production is attributed to coverage of more area under mango. The trend is shown in Table 3.7:

Table 3.7: Indices of Area, Production and Yield of Mango—India and World

Year	*World*			*India*		
	Area	*Production*	*Yield*	*Area*	*Production*	*Yield*
2004	100	100	100	100	100	100
2005	105	109	103	103	99	97
2006	113	109	101	107	108	100
2007	118	122	102	110	110	101
2008	123	131	106	113	113	101
2009	128	132	103	116	117	101
2010*	132	136	103	118	120	101
CAGR	**4.57**	**5.14**	**0.43**	**2.57**	**2.87**	**0.30**

*Provisional, Base Year 2004 =100, Source: FAO Data Base 2009, Compiled from absolute data.

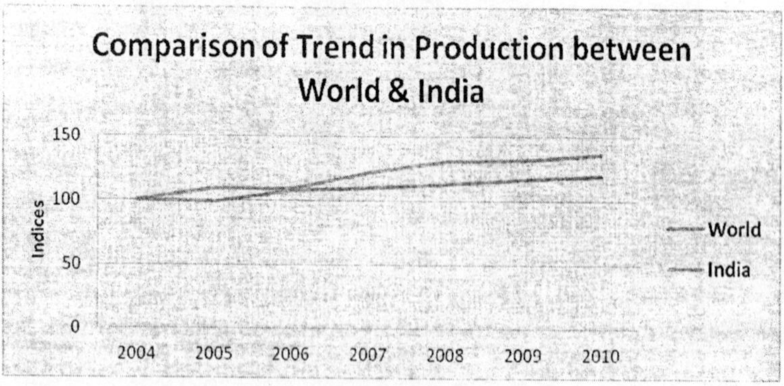

Graphic 3.9: Comparison of Production Trend of Mango –World

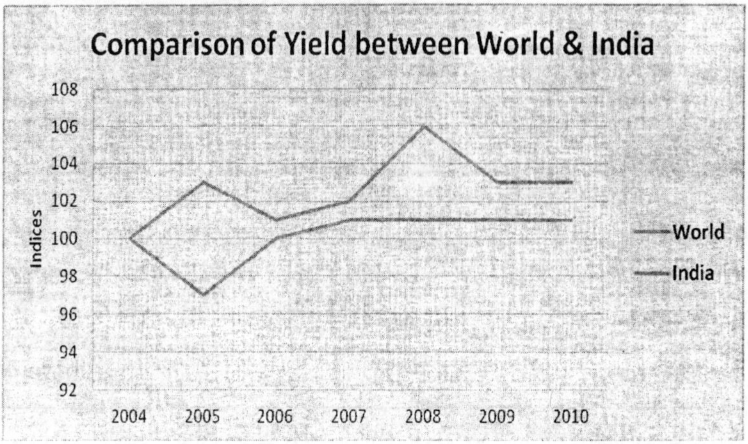

Graphic 3.10: Comparison of Productivity under Mango—World and India

On an average, area under mango in world increased by 4.57 per cent per year while in India it was 10 per cent per year. In case of production, world recorded an annual hike by 5.14 per cent compared to 2.87 per cent in India. Average annual growth rate of yield in world was only 0.43 per cent and in India it was 0.30 per cent.

3.8 State wise Scenario

The major mango growing states in India are Uttar Pradesh (UP), Gujarat, Andhra Pradesh (AP), Maharashtra, Orissa, Bihar, West Bengal, Karnataka, Goa, Haryana, Madhya Pradesh (MP), Punjab and Tamil Nadu. The region wise popular varieties grown in different parts of the country comprise Alphonso, Kesar from Western India, Banganpalli, Totapuri, and Neelam from Southern States, Fazli from Eastern State and Langra, Chausa and Dusheri from Northern States. Area wise, Andhra Pradesh occupies 21.55 per cent of the total area under mango in the country followed by Maharashtra (19.79%), Uttar Pradesh (11.74%), Bihar (6.2%), Karnataka (6.1%) etc.

3.9 Area under Mango in Major States

Area under mango in major states is given below:

Table 3.8: State wise Area under Mango during 1996-97 to 2008-09

Year	*AP*	*UP*	*Karnataka*	*Bihar*	*Maha-rashtra*	*W Bengal*	*Others*	*India*
1996-97	271.4	256.2	116.5	151.8	65.5	55.7	427.8	1344.9
2001-02	341.2	253.0	115.4	139.3	164.4	65.4	506.2	1575.8
2006-07	471.4	261.4	129.1	140.8	447.7	78.2	625.3	2153.9
2008-09	497.7	271.2	141.3	144.1	457.0	86.0	711.7	2309.0
CAGR	**6.94**	**0.49**	**1.77**	**-0.42**	**49.80**	**4.53**	**5.56**	**5.97**

Source: Indian Horticulture Data base 2009, Note— I= 1996-97, 2=2001-02, 3= 2006-07 and, 4= 2008-09, CAGR= Compounded annual growth rate.

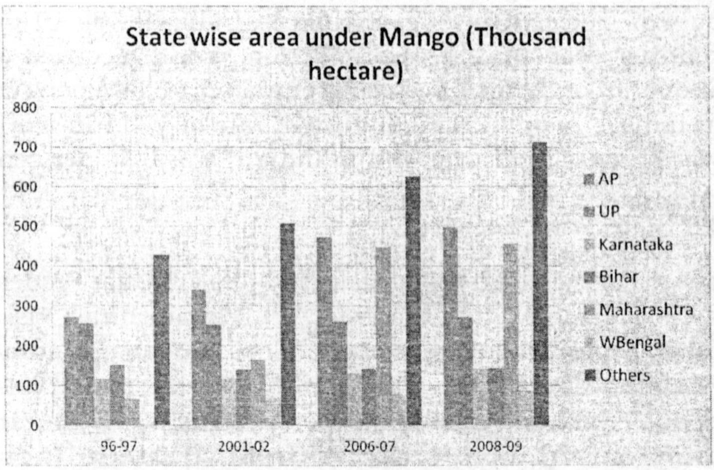

Graphic 3.11 State wise Area under Mango Cultivation

Compounded annual growth rate was 49.80 per cent in Maharashtra where as it was 6.94 per cent in Andhra Pradesh, 4.53 per cent in West Bengal and 1.77 per cent in Karnataka. CAGR of area under mango was 5.97 per cent for All India. The year-wise area under mango during

1996-97 to 2008-09 is furnished in **Annexure 5.**

In Andhra Pradesh production in 1996-97 recorded at 3256.3 thousand MT which increased 4445.8 thousand MT in 2001-02 and 3865 thousand MT in 2005-06. It, however, declined to 2522 thousand MT in 2008-09. In case of Uttar Pradesh there was a declining growth rate over four points of time. The trend was positive for other states (Table 3.9).

3.10 Production of Mango in Major States

Production of Mango in major states is given below:

Table 3.9: State-wise Production of Mango during 1996-97 to 2008-09

(Production in thousand MT)

Year	*AP*	*UP*	*Karnataka*	*Bihar*	*Maha-rashtra*	*W Bengal*	*Others*	*India*
1	3256.3	3548.0	1106.5	910.4	196.5	66.8	896.5	9981.0
2	4445.8	1950.4	1160.6	1253.5	559.6	585.0	2095.3	10020.2
3	3865.2	2980.5	1368.8	1306.9	646.3	549.8	3015.5	13734.0
4	2522.0	3465.9	1284.4	1329.8	714.8	548.9	2855.6	12749.8
CAGR	**-2.42**	**-0.19**	**1.34**	**3.84**	**21.9**	**4.53**	**60.14**	**2.31**

Source: Indian Horticulture Data base 2009, Note— I= 1996-97, 2=2001-02, 3= 2006-07 and, 4= 2008-09, CAGR= Compounded annual growth rate

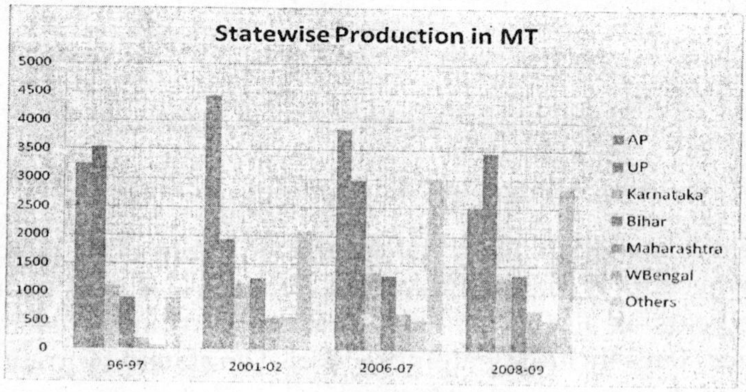

Graphic 3.12: Statewise Production of Mango

It transpired from the Table 3.10 that CAGR of mango production in Andhra Pradesh and Uttar Pradesh during the period from 1996-97 to 2008-09 was negative at 2.42 per cent 0.19 per cent respectively, while growth rate was very high (21.9%) in Maharashtra followed by West Bengal (4.53%), Bihar (3.84%) and Karnataka (1.34%). The year wise production of mango in states has been showcased in **Annexure 6.**

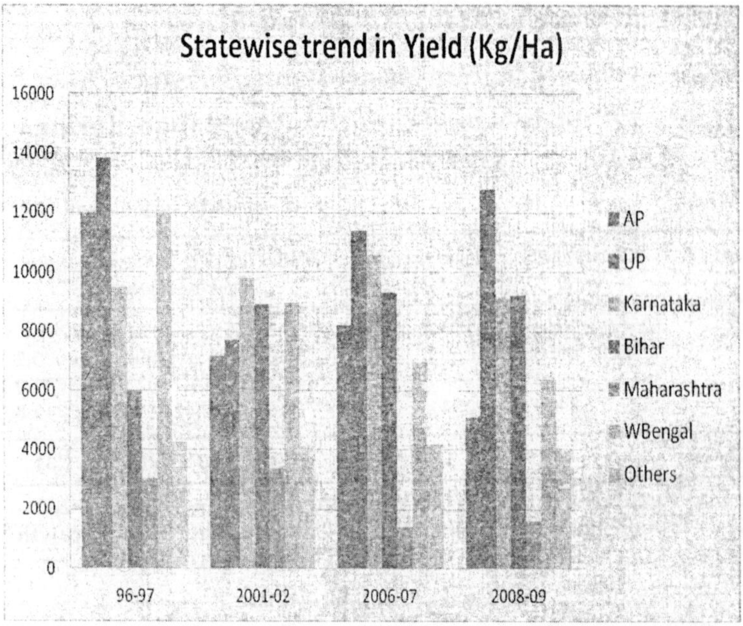

Graphic 3.13: State wise of Yield Mango

3.11 Yield of Mango in Major States

Yield of mango in major states depicted the fact that yield per hectare of mango in Andhra Pradesh declined over the years as also in Maharashtra, while it improved in other states including all India level. The state-wise trend of yield is presented below:

Table 3.10: Statewise Yield of Mango during 1996-97 to 2008-09

(Yield kg per hectare)

Year	*AP*	*UP*	*Karnataka*	*Bihar*	*Maha-rashtra*	*W Bengal*	*Others*	*India*
1	11980	13840	9500	5997	3000	12000	4270	7400
2	7170	7700	9800	8900	3400	8944	4141	6400
3	8220	11400	10600	9300	1400	7000	4184	6400
4	5100	12800	9100	9200	1600	6400	4050	5500
CAGR	**-10.37**	**-0.62**	**0.32**	**4.10**	**-16.34**	**6.73**	**0.40**	**-2.56**

Source: Indian Horticulture Data base 2009, Note— I= 1996-97, 2=2001-02, 3= 2006-07 and, 4= 2008-09, CAGR= Compounded annual growth rate

In Maharashtra the CAGR was negative at 16.34 per cent followed by Andhra Pradesh (-10.37%) and Uttar Pradesh (-0.62%). The CAGR of India was recorded at –2.56 per cent **(Annexure 7).**

3.12 Exports of Mango from India

The world trade in fresh mango forms an insignificant portion of world production (only 0.60 %). India's share in world mango market is less than 15 per cent but mangoes account for around 39 per cent of the total fruit exports from India (Muley). In the near future mango exports from India are likely to go up. During the period of 1994-95 to 2008-09 only 1.34 per cent of total mango production per year was exported from India. Currently around 95 per cent of India's mango exports are routed through Middle East countries. Given the strong consumers preference for Indian mangoes, well planned export and commodity promotion programme can help the country to achieve a dominant position in the world market. Data on exports of mango from India during 1994-95 to 2008-09 are presented in Table 3.11:

Table 3.11: Exports of Mango from India during 1994-95 to 2008-09

Year exports to	*Exports MT)*	*Value (in thousand Rs.)*	*Production (in crore MT)*	*Share of (in thousand product (%)*
1994-95	70.44	115.15	10993	0.54
1997-98	116.48	169.18	10234	1.13
2000-01	112.97	279.00	10057	1.12
2003-04	171.01	402.39	11490	1.49
2007-08	219.19	598.54	13997	1.56
2008-08	247.15	627.81	12750	1.33
Average	156.20	365.20	11586	1.34
CAGR(%)	**17.91**	**31.80**	**1.14**	-

Source:- APEDA, Indian Horticulture Data Base, 2009 and National Horticulture Board, @ fresh and Pulp

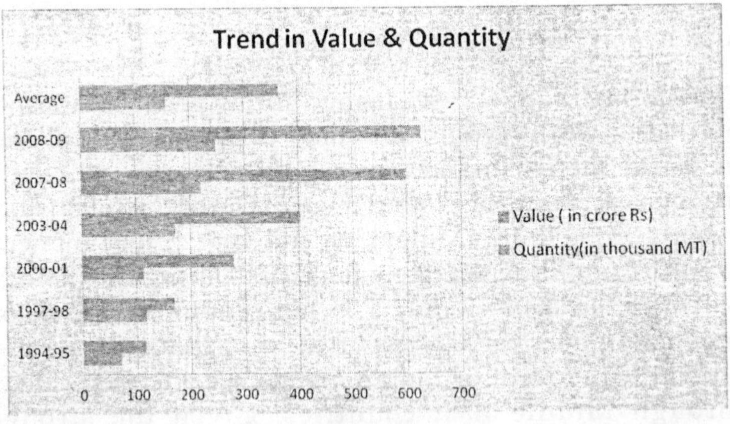

Graphic 3.14: Value and Quantity of Mango

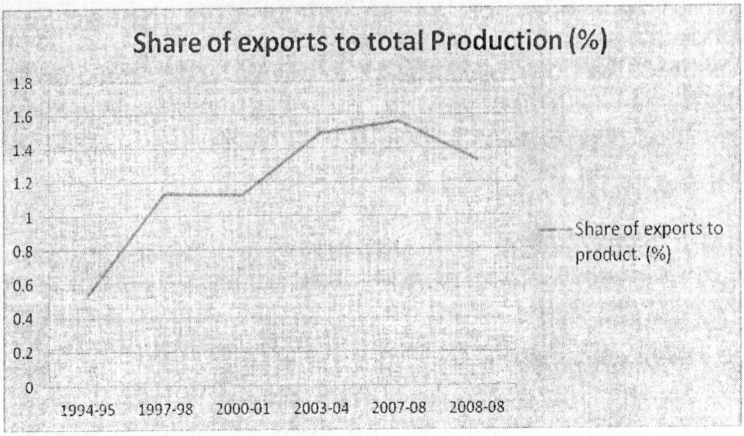

Graphic 3.15: Shares of Exports of Mango to Total Mango Production

On an average 156 thousand MT of mangoes of value Rs 365 crore per year including fresh and pulp was exported to many countries during the period of 1994-95 to 2008-09. Mangoes are mainly exported to Bangladesh (24 thousand MT), UAE (21 thousand MT), Saudi Arabia (4 thousand MT), Nepal (3 thousand MT), UK (1 thousand MT), and Russia (2 thousand MT). Export of mango accounts for 1.34 per cent of production per year over the period 1994-95 to 2008-09 (Table 3.11). Year-wise export of fresh mango and mango pulp is given in **Annexure 8.**

Speciality and Quality of Indian Mango: Indian mango is the special product that the high standards of quality and bountiful of nutrients packed in it. A single mango can provide up to 40 percent of the daily dietary fiber needs. In addition, this luscious fruit contains potassium, beta-carotene and antioxidants. In India, mangoes are mainly grown in tropical and subtropical regions from sea level to an altitude of 1,500m. Mangoes grow best in temperatures around 27°C. For maintaining highest quality standards, State-of-the-art pack-houses have been set up in major production zones. Keeping in view the different country's requirements, internationally recognized treatment facilities like Hot Water Treatment, Vapour Heat Treatment and Irradiation facilities have also been set up at various locations across the production belt. Unique product identification system, compliant to the traceability networking and Pesticide Residue Monitoring Plan have been developed for the consumer safety, and readiness to product recall in case of any emergency (health hazards).

3.13 Varieties

India is the home of about 1,000 varieties of mango. However, only a few varieties are commercially cultivated throughout India. Most of the Indian mango varieties have specific eco-geographical requirements for optimum growth and yield. The Northern/Eastern Indian varieties are usually late bearing compared to Southern and Western Indian varieties. Some of the local varieties of mango bear fruits throughout the year in extreme southern parts of India. The import and commerce of varities of mango are presented in Table 3.12.

Table 3.12: State-wise Commercial Varieties of Indian Mango

Andhra Pradesh:	Banganapalli, Suvarnarekha, Neelum and Totapuri
Bihar:	Bombay Green, Chausa, Dashehari, Fazli, Gulabkhas, Kishen Bhog, Himsagar, Zardalu and Langra
Gujarat:	Kesar, Alphonso, Rajapuri, Jamadar, Totapuri, Neelum, Dashehari and Langra
Haryana:	Chausa, Dashehari, Langra and Fazli
Himachal Pradesh:	Chausa, Dashehari and Langra
Karnataka:	Alphonso, Totapuri, Banganapalli, Pairi, Neelum and Mulgoa
Madhya Pradesh:	Alphonso, Bombay Green, Dashehari, Fazli, Langra and Neelum
Maharashtra:	Alphonso, Kesar and PairiPunjabChausa, Dashehari and Malda
Rajasthan:	Bombay Green, Chausa, Dashehari and Langra
Tamil Nadu:	Alphonso, Totapuri, Banganapalli and Neelum
Uttar Pradesh:	Bombay Green, Chausa, Dashehari and Langra
West Bengal:	Fazli, Gulabkhas, Himsagar, Kishenbhog, Langra and Bombay Green

4

Trends in Area, Production, and Yield of Mango in Selected States Vis a Vis All India

This chapter deals with production and productivity of mango in selected states. While deliberating on this subject various issues on low productivity, absence of storage facility, non availability of adequate quality of raw material at reasonable prices, lack of value addition, poor back ward and forward linkages may come and those were dwelt upon in subsequent chapters.

4.1 Area under Mango Cultivation—India and Selected States

Area under mango cultivations during 1996-97 to 2008-09 is shown in the Table 4.1.

Of the selected states, Andhra Pradesh covered an area of 271.4 thousand hectares under mango representing 69.1 per cent in 1996-97, while it was 65.5 thousand hectares (16.7%) for Maharashtra and 55.7 thousand hectare (14.2%) for West Bengal. Area under mango cultivation went up to 497.5 thousand hectares (83%) in Andhra Pradesh, 457 thousand hectares in Maharashtra

(597%) and 86 thousand hectares in (54.4%) during 2008-09. It is interesting to note that percentage increase in area under mango cultivation in selected states was higher (165%) than All India (71%).

Table 4.1: Area under Mango cultivation during 1996-97 to 2008-09—India and Selected States

(Area in thousand hectare)

State/ Year	*1996-97*	*Percent to total*	*2006-07*	*Percent to total*	*2008-09*	*Percent to total*	*% increase over 1996-97*
A. Pradesh	271.4	69.1	471.4	47.3	497.5	47.8	83
Maharashtra	65.5	16.7	447.1	44.9	457.0	43.9	597
West Bengal	55.7	14.2	78.2	7.8	86.0	8.3	54
Selected states	**392.6**	**100.0**	**996.7**	**100.0**	**1040.7**	**100.0**	**165**
All India	**1344.9**	**23.1**	**2153.9**	**45.2@**	**2309.0@**	**45.4**	**71**

Source: Indian Horticulture Data base 2009, @ percent of area under mango in selected states to All India area.

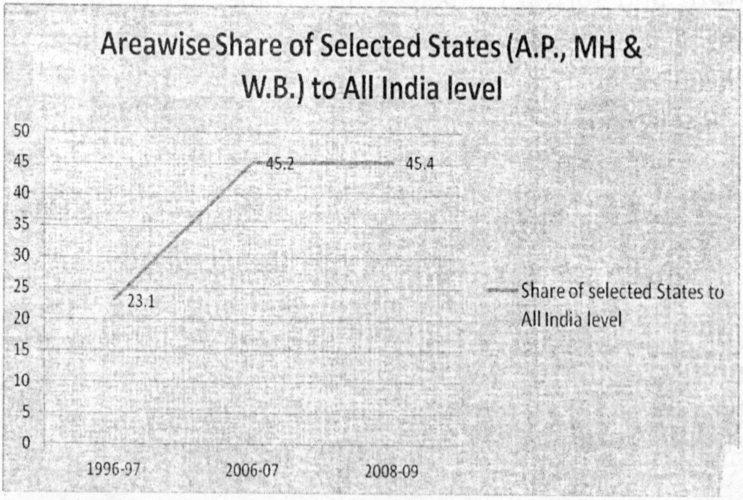

Graphic 4.1: Share of Area under Mango in Selected States to All India

4.2 Production of Mango—India and Selected States

Production of mango for selected state in 1996-97 stood at 3514.6 thousand MT which increased to 3783.7 thousand MT (269.1 thousand MT) in 2008-09. This was attributed to hike of production in Maharashtra by 516.3 thousand MT and West Bengal by 482.1 thousand MT and a shortfall of production in Andhra Pradesh by 743.3 thousand MT and. The position is portrayed in Table 4.2:

Table 4.2: Production of Mango during 1996-97 to 2008-09—India and Selected States

(Production in thousand metric ton—MT)

State/ Year	*1996-97*	*Percent to total*	*2006-07*	*Percent to total*	*2008-09*	*Percent to total*	*Percent increase over 1996-97*
Andhra Pradesh	3256.3	92.6	3865.0	76.4	2522.0	66.6	-22.6
Maharashtra	196.5	5.6	646.3	12.8	712.8	18.8	262.7
West Bengal	66.8	1.8	549.8	10.8	548.9	14.6	721.7
Selected states	**3519.6**	**100.0**	**5061.1**	**100.0**	**3783.7**	**100.0**	**7.7**
All India	**9981.2**	**35.2@**	**13734.0**	**35.8@**	**12749.8**	**29.7@**	**27.8**

Source: Indian Horticulture Data Base 2009, @ Percent of production of mango of selected states to All India production.

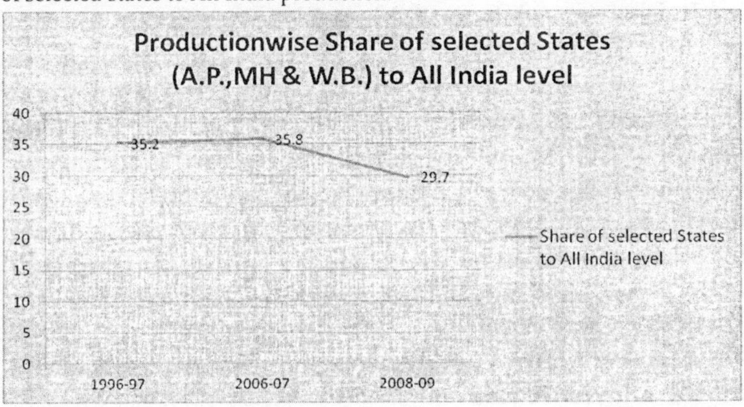

Graphic 4.2 Share of Production in Selected States to All India

In 1996-97 selected states contributed 35.2 per cent of total production of mango in India. The share was almost same in 2006-07 (35.8%). It, however, went down by 29.7 per cent in 2008-09. Percentage increase in production was on lower side at 7.7 per cent compared to All India (27.8%).

4.3 Productivity of Mango—India and Selected States

Table 4.3: Productivity of Mango during 1996-97 to 2008-09—India and Selected States

(Productivity in kg per hectare)

State/ Year	*1996-97*	*2006-07*	*2008-09*	*Increase/ decrease in absolute terms*	*Percent increase over 1996-97*
Andhra Pradesh	11,980	8,200	5,100	- 6,850	-57.1
Maharashtra	3,000	1,400	1,600	- 1,400	-46.7
West Bengal	12,000	7,000	6,400	-5,600	-46.7
Selected states	**8,964**	**5,078**	**3,635**	**-5,329**	**-59.4**
All India	**7,400**	**6,400**	**5,550**	**-1,900**	**-25.7**

Source: Indian Horticulture Data base 2009, @ Percent of yield of mango of selected states to All India yield.

It is observed from Table 4.3 above that in Andhra Pradesh productivity of mango declined by 6,850 kg per hectare between 1996-97 and 2008-09. The same trend was noticed for Maharashtra (1,400 per hectare) and West Bengal (5,600 kg per hectare). The fall in productivity was high at 5329 kg per hectare in selected states compared to All India (1900 kg per hectare). Productivity went down by 59.4 per cent in selected states against All India fall of 25.7 per cent between 1996-97 and 2008-09.

4.4 Year Wise Area under Mango Cultivation—Sample States and All India

Year wise data on area under mango cultivation depicted

the fact there was sharp rise in area in all the three states. The CAGR of area in Maharashtra stood at 49.8% followed by Andhra Pradesh (6.9 %) and West Bengal (4.5 %) .There is an increasing trend in area under mango cultivation in all the selected states. Total area under mango cultivation in the selected states as a whole showed an increase by 65 per cent compared to All India figure of 71 per cent. **Annexure 9 showed** the details.

4.5 Year Wise Production of Mango—Sample States and All India

Production of mango in Andhra Pradesh declined during the year. It was maximum at 4157 thousand MT in 2007-08 and minimum at 2269.6 thousand MT in 1998-99.The cumulative annual growth rate recorded at -1.87 per cent. In case Maharashtra production level varied from 196.5 thousand MT to 712.8 thousand MT accounting for a compound growth rate of 21.9 per cent. For West Bengal the compound annual growth rate was 60.14 per cent. The growth rate of selected states was 9.0 per cent which was lower than All India growth rate of 10.7 per cent. **Annexure 10** clarified the position.

4.6 Year Wise Yield of Mango—Sample States and All India

Year wise yield of Andhra Pradesh showed a declining trend. The trend was similar for both Maharashtra and West Bengal. All three states showed negative growth rate. The growth rate of the selected states registered at – 4.3 per cent compared to All India average of - 6.2 per cent. **Annexure 11** provided the clear picture.

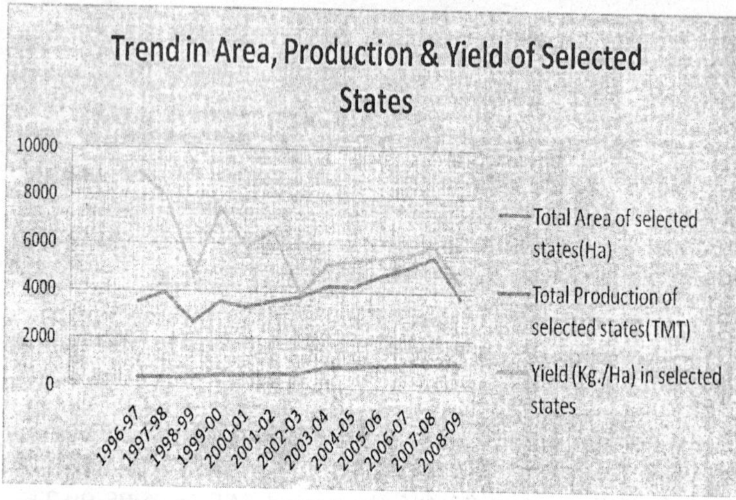

Graphic 4.3: Area, Production and Yield of Mango in Selected States

In Andhra Pradesh the yield rate in all the years' expect 1996-97 (12,000 per kg) started falling. The fall was very sharp in 2008-09 (5100 kg per hectare). The compounded annual growth rate stood at -4.8 per cent. In Maharashtra there was a declining trend of growth rate of productivity. It was lowest in 1997-98 (1000 kg/ha). The CAGR recorded at -3.98 per cent. The picture was same for West Bengal. The CAGR registered at -3.89.

4.7 Area, Production and Yield of Mango in Selected Districts of Andhra Pradesh

Mango is presently cultivated in 22 districts of Andhra Pradesh. Chittor district occupied an area of 58.9.thousand hectares and Krishna disctrict 80.4 thousand hectares in 2008-09 accounting for 28.8 per cent of total area in Andhra Pradesh. Chittor district also produces mango to the level of 508.7 thousand MT and Krishna district 607.5 thousand MT and both constituting 44.25 of total production of Andhra Pradesh. Year wise area, production and yield in Chittor district are shown in the **Annexure 12**. Area and production of Krishna district were 80.4 thousand hectares and 607.5 thousand MT respectively (Table 4.4). Year wise area, production and yield of Krishna district are presented in **Annexure 13.**

Table 4.4: Area, Production and Yield of Mango in Selected Districts and Andhra Pradesh

District/year	*Area (thousand hectare)*		*Production (thousand MT)*		*Yield (kg/ hectare)*	
	1998-99	*2008-09*	*1998-99*	*2008-09*	*1998-99*	*2008-09*
Chittor	33.0	58.9	106.8	508.7	3236	8636
Krishna	61.2	80.4	803.4	607.5	13127	7576
Sub total	**94.2**	**139.3**	**910.2**	**1116.2**	**9662**	**8011**
Share @(%)	**33.4**	**28.8**	**40.1**	**44.25**	**662**	**2911**

Source: Directorate of Economics and Statistics, Govt. of Andhra Pradesh.
@ Percentage of two districts to total Andhra Pradesh.

Yield of mango in Krishna district is higher (13,127 kg /ha) than Chittor (3,236 kg/ha). Taking both the districts, the yield rate in 1998-99 was worked out at 9,662 kg per hectare which is higher by 662 kg/ha compared to Andhra Pradesh (9,000 kg/ha) in 1998-99. The productivity was higher to the level of 2,911 kg/ha in 2008-09 as against 5,100 kg per hectare of Andhra Pradesh in 2008-09 **(Annexure 14)**. The Year wise share of area and production, of these two **selected districts vis a vis Andhra Pradesh** has been figured in **Annexure 15**

4.8 Major Mango Producing Districts of Maharashtra

Major mango producing districts in Maharashtra are indicated in table below:

Table 4.5: Area, Production and Yield of Mango in Major Districts of Maharashtra during 2008-09

(Area in hectare, Production in ton and yield in kg per hectare)

District	Area under Mango	Share (%)	Production	Share (%)	Yield
Ratnagiri	43616	10.24	117351	18.63	3400
Raigad	41586	9.77	81826	12.99	3390
Thane	37289	8.76	70258	11.16	3400
Sindhudurg	23267	5.46	53871	8.55	3390
Pune	16533	3.88	47416	7.53	3399
Ahmedanagar	20796	4.88	24384	3.87	3399
Nanded	17734	4.16	34761	5.52	3399
Aurangabad	15109	3.55	14741	2.34	3399
Other Districts	209870	49.30	185192	29.40	883
Total of Maharashtra	**425800**	**100.00**	**629800**	**100.00**	**3400**

Source: Directorate of Horticulture, Govt.of Maharashtra.

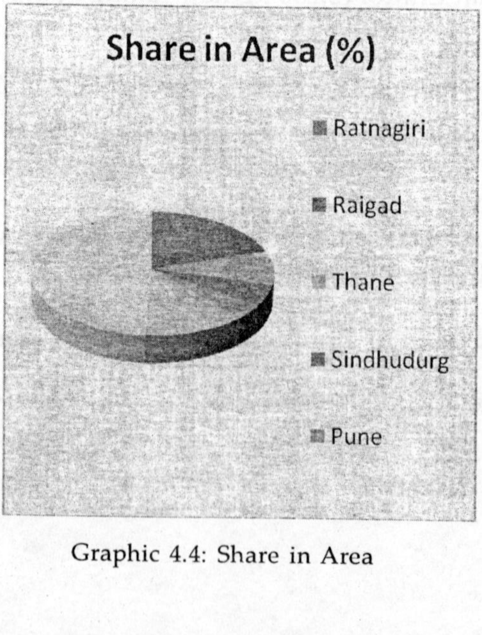

Graphic 4.4: Share in Area

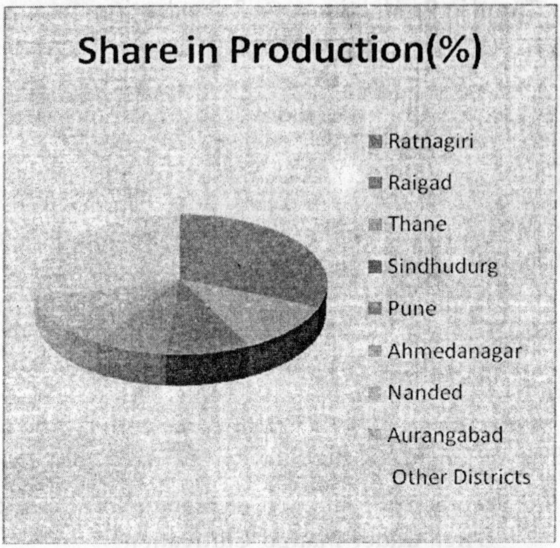

Graphic 4.5: Share in Production

Ratnagiri district contributes 10 and 18 per cent of the mango area and production, respectively. The yield in Ratnagiri is same (3400 kg /ha) with that of the state as a whole. All these major mango producing districts of Maharashtra have more or less similar yield as compared with state average. It lends support to the fact that increase in the area under nontraditional regions of the state may have decreased the average yield of the state.

4.9 Cultivation of Mango in Selected Districts of Maharashtra

Area under mango cultivation in Maharashtra has been continuously rising over the years. Production, however, has been declining due to decline in yield. The production in the selected district of **Sindhudurg** of Maharashtra has been increasing over the years mainly due to the rise in productive area. The compounded annual growth rate of area stood at 1.98 per cent, while it was 8.64 per cent for production and -2.35 per cent for yield. (**Annexure 16.**)

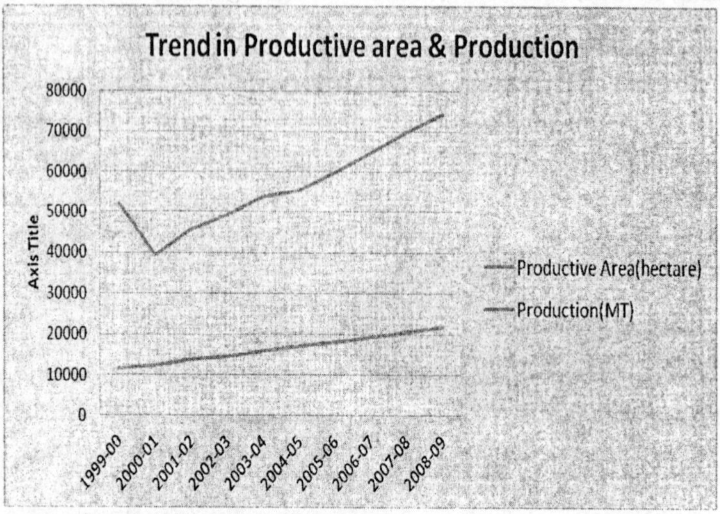

Graphic 4.6: Trends in Production of Mango and Productive Area under Mango Cultivation

The areas adjacent to the sea shore give early and better yield of Alphonso mango. Therefore Alphonso cultivation is more popular in Devgad, Malvan and Vengurle Talukas of the district. In the recent years cultivation of the mango has spread throughout the district. The taluka wise area under mango cultivation is indicated in Table 4.6:

Table 4.6: Taluka-wise Area under Mango Cultivation in Sindhudurg in 2008-09

Name of the Block	*Area in hectare*	*Per cent to total*
Devgad	7,980	33.26
Malvan	4,138	17.25
Vengurle	3,431	14.30
Kudal	2,755	11.47
SawantWadi	2,525	10.52
Kankavali	2,495	10.40
Vaibhavwadi	668	2.80
Total	**23,992**	**100.00**

Source: Directorate of Horticulture, Govt.of Maharashtra.

The production in **Sindhudurg** has been increasing over the years due mainly to the rise in productive area. The compounded growth rate of area stood at 1.98 per cent, while it was 8.64 per cent in production area and -2.35 per cent in yield per hectare. The yield is not declining in the district. However, the yield of Mango at 3400 kg in Sindhudurg disctrict of Maharashtra per hectare is very low in comparison to all India average of 5500 kg per hectare.

In **Aurangabad district**, cultivation of Kesar variety of mango is a recent development. It is gathered from the field study that oldest Kesar mango orchard in the district, so also in the state, is about 20 years old. However, in view of the better price available to farmers in growing Kesar Mango, more and more number of orchards are coming up in the district. On a rough estimate, 5-10 per cent of the mango trees in the district constitute Kesar variety. Aurangabad, Paithan and Kannad are the major Kesar mango growing talukas in the district. Year wise data relating to area, production and yield is depicted in **Annexure 17.**

4.10 Cultivation of Mango in Selected Districts of West Bengal

Mango is one of the most popular fruits of **Malda district.** About 250 varieties of mango are grown in the district, in comparison to 1,100-1,200 varieties in the country. Mango was cultivated in 26,400 hectares in 2009 with annual production of 19, 02,000 MT. The average size of mango orchard was 0.23 hectare. The average productivity stood at 7,204 kg per hectare in Malda. The CAGR of area, production and productivity was recorded at 0.76 per cent, 10.86 per cent and 8.02 per cent respectively. Area, Production and productivity related data of mango during 1990-2008 are furnished in **Annexure 18.** There are 10 mango growing blocks in Malda district. Out of this English Bazar devoted 9156 hectare accounting for 34.56 per cent of total area under mango followed by Ratua II (2,542 hectares) and Ratua I (2,540 hectares). In terms of production English Bazar ranks first (46,335kg), Ratua II stood second (28,986 kg) and Manik Chak reckoned third (27,412 kg). The information on mango growing blocks of Malda is given in **Annexure 19.**

Murshidabad district is famous for its quality mangoes. Mango orchards occupy a sizeable area in Murshidabad district. More than 85 varieties of mangoes are grown in the district of which 33 are commercially important. Most of them are famous for their taste and quality. Those were liked by Nawab Nizams of Subey Bengal. The various commonly grown commercial varieties are *Rani Pasand, Bombai, Bimli, Biara, Bhababi, Bariha, Fazli, Golapkhas, Golapbhog, Anaras, Champa, Molaemjam, Himsagar, Sadoulla, Nabab Pasand, Mohanbhog, Langra, Surma Fazli, Chausa, Kalapahar, Kohitoor, Neelam etc..* Recently introduced varieties are Mallika and AmraPalli. Total area in the district was 15587 hectare with an annual production of 126102 metric ton in 2009. Average yield was 7937 kg per hectare. Average size of mango orchard was 0.25 hectare. There are 13 important blocks are there where mango is grown. Lalgola, Suti-II, and Jiaganj blocks constituted 19.79 per cent, 19.69 per cent and 16.62 percent of total area of the district, respectively. In terms of production all three blocks accounted for 17.82 per cent, 17.32 per cent and 15.62 per cent respectively. Data relating to area, production etc of the mango growing blocks of Murshidabad district are furnished in **Annexure 20.**

5

Profile of Mango Growers and Mango Orchards

This chapter confines to the profile of sample mango growers (farmers) in selected three states mainly Andhra Pradesh, Maharashtra and West Bengal. The analysis is based on certain parameters like age, level of education, social status, occupational pattern, size of family etc. Attempt has also made to classify the mango orchards according to land holding.

5.1 Age Wise Classification of Mango Growers/Farmers

As many 31 sample farmers constituting 33.7 per cent of the total sample (92) belongs to the age group of 36-45 years and 30 sample farmers accounting for 32.6 percent in the age group of 26-35 years and 19 farmers representing 20.7 per cent in the age bracket of 20-25 years. There is only 1 farmer who attained the age above 55 years. State wise picture revealed that in Maharashtra 20 farmers had an age between 26 and 35 years and 14 in the range of 36 to 45 years. Table below shows the details.

Table 5.1: Age wise Distribution of Sample Mango Growers

Age/State	*AP@*	*Per cent*	*Mahar@*	*Per cent*	*W B@*	*P. Cent@*	*Total@*	*Per cent*
20-25	5	11.9	10	25.0	4	40.0	19	20.7
26-35	20	47.6	06	15.0	4	40.0	30	32.6
36-45	14	33.3	15	37.5	2	20.0	31	33.7
46-55	02	4.7	09	22.5	-	-	11	12.0
55 & Above	01	0.8	-	-	-	-	01	1.0
Row Total	**42**	**100.0**	**40**	**100.0**	**10**	**100.**	**92**	**100**

Source: Field Data, @ Number of Sample Mango Growers/Farmers

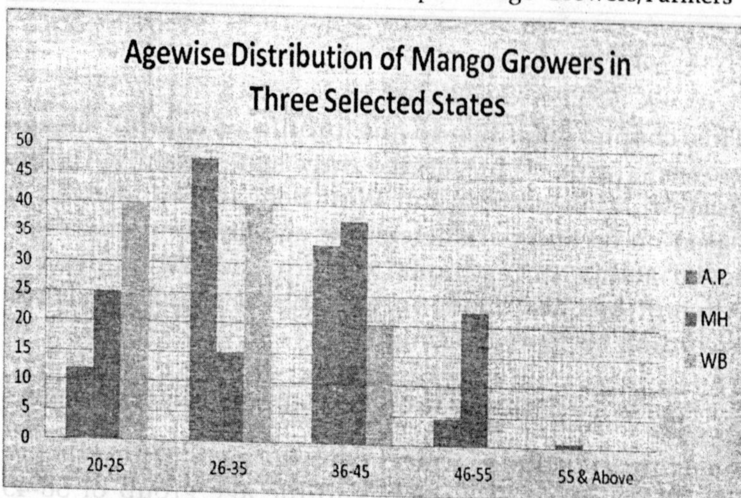

Graphic 5.1: Distributions of Mango Growers by Age

5.2 Classification of Mango Growers/Farmers by Level of Education

Mango farmers have been categorized according to the level of education. Of the total 92 mango growers, 32 farmers representing 34.8 per cent of the total passed higher secondary. Fifty eight farmers accounting for 63.00 per cent attained education up to secondary level. Only two farmers were graduates. The state wise position revealed that expect West Bengal, 10 per cent and 24 per cent of the sample farmers in Andhra Pradesh and Maharashtra had primary education respectively. Table below outlines the details.

Table 5.2: Distribution of Sample Mango Growers by level of Education

Level of Education	*AP@*	*Per cent*	*Mahar@*	*Per cent*	*W B@*	*P. Cent@*	*Total@*	*Per cent*
Primary	4	9.5	10	24.0	4	40.0	18	19.6
Post Primary	6	14.3	06	15.0	3	30.0	15	16.3
Secondary	12	28.6	10	25.0	3	30.0	25	27.1
Higher Secondary	18	42.9	14	35.0	-	-	32	34.8
Degree	02	5.1	-	-	-	-	02	2.2
Row Total	**42**	**100.0**	**40**	**100.0**	**10**	**100.0**	**92**	**100.0**

Source: Field Data, @ Number of Sample Mango Growers.

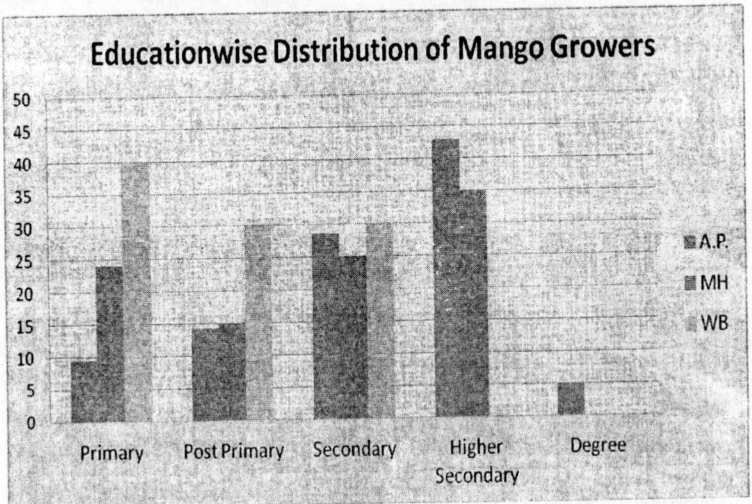

Graphic 5.2: Distributions of Mango Growers by Level of Education

5.3 Classification of Mango Growers/ Farmers by Social Group

Majority of the mango growers (52.2 %) belonged to general cast. About one third of the total samples ie 33.7 per cent were in the category of OBC. Samples belonging to SC /ST and minority category constituted only 16 per cent. State-wise the picture was same.

Table 5.3: Distributions of Sample Mango Growers by Social Group

Social Group	AP@	Per cent	Mahar@	Per cent	W B@	P. Cent@	Total@	Per cent
General	20	47.6	22	55.0	06	60.0	48	52.2
OBC	14	33.3	14	35.0	03	30.	31	33.7
SC/ST	06	14.3	-	-	-	-	06	06.5
Minority	02	4.8	4	10.0	01	10.	07	09.6
Row Total	**42**	**100.**	**40**	**100.0**	**10**	**100.0**	**92**	**100.0**

Source: Field Data, @ Number of Sample Mango Growers.

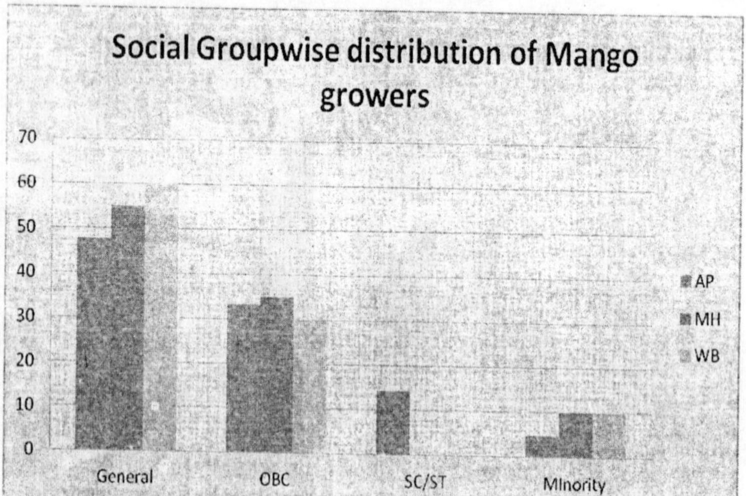

Graphic 5.3: Distributions of Mango Growers by Social Group

5.4 Classification of Mango Growers/ Farmers by Family Size

Out of a total of 92 samples, only 17 samples forming 18.5 per cent had a family size up to 3 members. As many as 40 samples had a family size between 4 and 6. State wise sample growers with family size between 4 and 6in Andhra Pradesh stood at 75.5 per cent followed by Maharashtra (62.5) and West Bengal (50%). Table 5.4 clarifies the position.

Table 5.4: Distribution of Sample Mango Growers by Size of Family

Size of Family	*AP@*	*Per cent*	*Mahar@*	*Per cent*	*W B@P.*	*Cent@*	*Total@*	*Per cent*
Up to 3	9	20.5	10	25.0	02	20.0	17	18.5
04-06	32	75.5	25	62.5	05	50.0	40	43.5
07 & above	01	4.0	05	12.5	03	30.0	35	38.0
Row Total	**42**	**100.**	**40**	**100.0**	**10**	**100.0**	**92**	**100.0**

Source: Field Data, @ Number of Sample of Mango Growers.

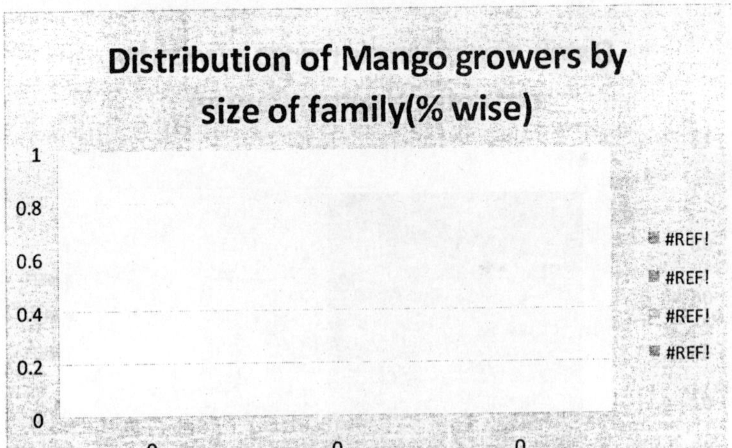

Graphic 5.4: Distribution of Mango Growers by Family Size

5.5 Classification of Mango Growers/ Farmers by Occupational Pattern

Distribution of occupational pattern of the sample growers observed that business man constituted 43.5 percent (40) of the total followed by traders accounting for 38.0 per cent (35) and cultivators 18.5 percent (17). Business man and traders dominate (81.5 %) mango sector. The State wise the same trend is noticed (Table 5.5).

Table 5.5: Distributions of Sample Mango Growers by Occupational Pattern

Occupation	*AP@*	*Per cent*	*Mahar@*	*Per cent*	*W B@P.*	*Cent@*	*Total@*	*Per cent*
Cultivation	10	23.8	05	12.5	2	20.0	17	18.5
Business	20	47.6	15	37.5	5	50.0	40	43.5
Trading	12	28.6	20	50.5	3	30.0	35	38.0
Row Total	**42**	**100.0**	**40**	**100.0**	**10**	**100.0**	**92**	**100.0**

Source: Field Data, @ Number of Sample of Mango Growers.

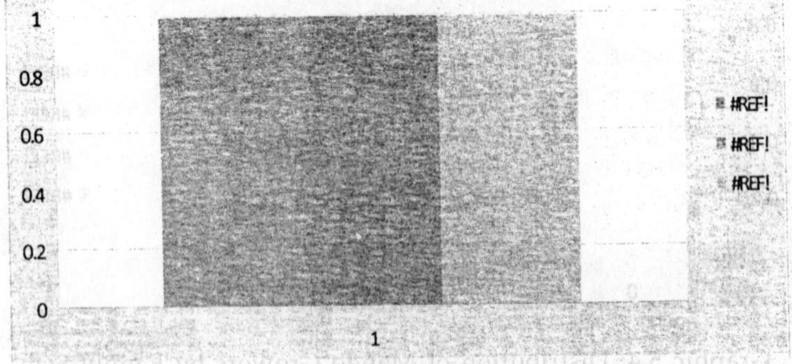

Graphic 5.5: Distribution of Mango Growers by Occupational Pattern

5.6 Classification of Sample Mango Growers by Size of Land Holding

Twenty one samples representing 22.8 per cent of the total had a landholding size between 10.01 and 20 acres followed by 20 samples in the land holding of 5.01 to 10 acres. About 22 sample growers accounting for 23.9 per cent belonged to land holding up to 5 acres (Table 5.6).

Table 5.6: Size Wise Distributions of Sample Mango Orchards

Size of land holding	*AP@*	*Per cent*	*Mahar@*	*Per cent*	*W B@*	*P. Cent@*	*Total@*	*Per cent*
Below 2.5Acr	2	4.8	4	10.0	2	20	08	8.6
2.5-5.0 Acr	8	19..0	4	10.0	2	20.0	14	15.3
5.01-10 Acr	13	32.0	5	12.5	2	20.0	20	21.8
10.01-25 Acr	15	35.7	5	12.5	1	10.0	21	22.8
25.01-50 Acr	4	9.5	22	55.0	3	30.0	09	31.3
Row Total	**42**	**100.0**	**40**	**100.0**	**10**	**100.0**	**92**	**100.0**

Source: Field Data, Number of Sample Mango Orchards (Farms)

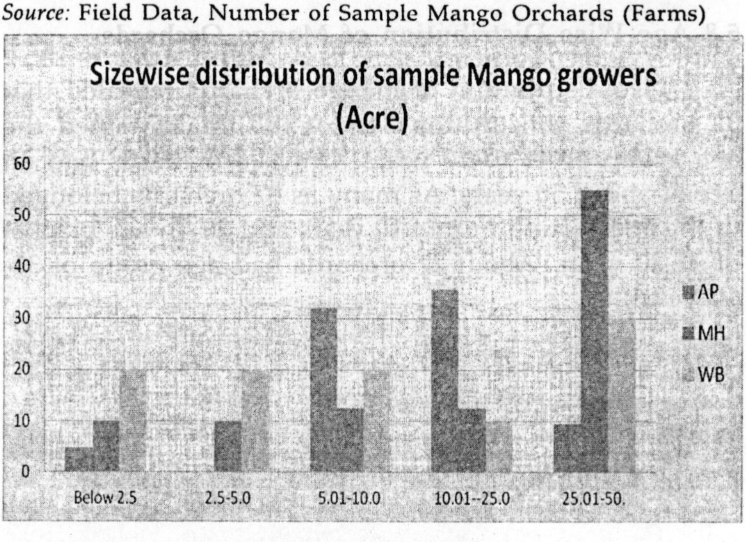

Graphic 5.6: Distribution of Mango Growers by Acreage

5.7 Distribution of Mango Growers by Acreage of Land

Total area covered under mango plantation for the sample growers was arrived at 1452.4 acres. Out of which 46.1 per cent (666.9 acres) belonged to the size class of 10.01 to 25 acres followed by 30.8 per cent in the size class of 25.01 to 50 acres and 18.3 per cent in the size class of 5.01 to 10 acres (Table 5.7).

Table 5.7: Area wise Distribution of Sample Mango Orchards

Size in Acre	*AP@*	*Per cent*	*Mahar@*	*Per cent*	*W B@*	*P. Cent@*	*Total@*	*Per cent*
Below 2.5	4.5	0.9	2.0	0.6	5.0	0.8	11.5	0.8
2. 51 to 5.0	32.5	5.7	-	-	25.0	3.8	57.5	4.0
5.01 to 10.0	117.5	20.6	13.0	6.0	135.5	20.7	266.0	18.3
10.01 to 25.0	303.5	53.4	6.0	2.6	360.4	54.9	669.0	46.1
25.01 to 50.0	110.5	19.4	207.0	9.8	130.5	19.8	447.5	30.8
Row Total	**568.0**	**100.0**	**228.0**	**100.0**	**656.4**	**100.0**	**1452.4**	**100**

Source: Field data, @ Number sample Farms, P.C= Per cent

5.8 Age Wise Distribution of Mango Orchards

Age wise distribution of mango orchards revealed that 32 orchards constituting 34.8 of the total attained the age group of 41 to 50 years. Only 06 orchards had an age of above 50 years. As many as 07 orchards belonged to the age group of up to 10 years and 20 in age bracket of 11-20 years. About 27 orchards had age group of 31-40 years.

Table 5.8: Distribution of Sample Mango Orchards by Age

Age Group	*AP@*	*Per cent*	*Mahar@*	*Per cent*	*W B@*	*P. Cent@*	*Total@*	*Per cent*
Upto 10 years	4	9.5	3	7.5	-	-	7	7.6
11 to 20	3	7.1	3	7.5	4	40.0	10	10.9
21 to 30	4	9.5	4	10.0	2	20.0	10	10.9
31 to 40	13	31.0	12	30.0	2	20.0	27	29.3
41 to 50	18	42.9	13	32.5	1	10.0	32	34.8
Above 50	-	-	05	12.5	1	10.0	06	6.5
Row Total	**42**	**100.0**	**40**	**100.0**	**10**	**100.0**	**92**	**100.0**

Source: Field Data, @ Number sample Farms.

6

Cultivation and Cultural Practices of Mango Orchard

This chapter deals with various cultivation practices like land preparation, digging of pits, preparation of drainage, sapling plantation, inter cropping, cover tree etc. while cultural practices includes application of manure, fertilizer, irrigation, spraying, weed/pest control, etc.

6.1 Land Preparation

Usually, all types of soil are conducive to mango cultivation. However, high, medium high land with exposure to sunlight throughout the day and having alluvium or fertile soil should be identified. The depth of soil should be 2-2.5 m. The sand, stones, pebbles, hard layer or soda containing layers at a depth of 1-1.5 may be removed for growth of plants. Inadequate food and water affects the growth and productivity decreases, fruits drop prematurely and the trees dry up. There should be adequate water drainage system and irrigation facilities during summer and winter seasons.

If the land is used for cultivation for the first time, uneven or full of weeds, then it has to be made cultivable by removing the weeds and by leveling of the land. In the month of June, seeds @ 50 kgs. per hectare may be sown. When the plants are around 30-40 days old, they should be thoroughly mixed with the soil using plough so that the decay enhances the fertility of the soil. During the next summer, pits of specified depth need to be dug. Distance between pits should be fixed depending on the mango variety and fertility of the soil. The soil of the upper and lower level of the pit should be exposed to adequate sunlight for 15-25 days. This results in the destruction of various insects present in the soil. Before plantation of the saplings, 40-50 kgs. Cow-dung or compost, 2.5 kgs. mustard or *neemkhol,* 500 gms. super phosphate and 25 gms 2 per cent folidol powder should be mixed with the soil of the pit and thereafter the pit may be filled with soil.

6.2 Sapling Plantation

Grafted clean healthy sapling having a straight shoot with green leaves should be identified for planting. Ideal time for planting of saplings is from mid June to mid September, i.e. during monsoon. In areas prone to flood or heavy rainfall, saplings should be sown at the end of the monsoon season and in areas prone to low rainfall, it must be sown at the beginning of the monsoon season. It is advised to plant/ sow the saplings in the evening. Nearly, 400 plants of crossbred variety per hectare for 5 m X 5 m distance and 82 plants of indigenous variety per hectare for 11 m X 11 m. distance may be planted.

Table 6.1: Number of Saplings

	Distance	*Measurement of the Pit*
Amrapali, Mallika, Neelum	5 mtr. X 5 mtr.	75 cm X 75 cm X 75 cm
Any indigenous variety (Himsagar,Fajli, Laxmanbhog etc.)	11 mtr. X 11 mtr.	1 mtr. X 1 mtr. X 1 mtr.

Ideal for mango plantation will be 18-20 trees per acre, which will ensure sufficient sunlight, production and color, quantity of the fruit. The ideal spacing between two plants is required to be 20 meters. However, at present it is found that 30 trees are planted per acre with an idea of increasing production per acre. But production in such cases is found to decrease after 8 - 10 years because the garden becomes congested and there will be lack of sunlight.

There are many methods of plantation - square, rectangle, polygon, etc. But square method is the most popular and easiest. Selected grafted sapling should be removed from earthen pot or polythene packs carefully. Care should be taken so that soil from the root does not break or come off. Then the saplings should be planted straight at the center of pits already mixed with fertilizer by removing 8-10 cm of soil. Thereafter, the loose soil should be lightly pressed around the sapling by hand to ensure that there is no gap at the base of the sapling. The growth will be affected if water or air gets through. The soil at the base of the sapling should be high so that no rainwater can accumulate at the spot. It is advisable to provide some support in the form of sticks which help them grow straight and strong. After plantation, water should be poured on the plant. It is advisable to plant the sapling at a specified distance in block or line. This ensures production round the year in the same orchard.

6.3 Post-Plantation Nursing

During winter and summer young plants are watered frequently to ensure proper growth. In case of adult trees, irrigation at 10-15 days interval from fruit set to maturity is beneficial for improving yield. However, irrigation is not recommended for 2-3 months prior to flowering as it is likely to promote vegetative growth at the expense of flowering. It is advisable to provide little irrigation regularly during winter and summer season. Also **provision of irrigation** to saplings up to five years is necessary as per details given below:

Table 6.2: Provision of Irrigation to Saplings up to Five Years

Provision of Irrigation/ Age of Sapling	*Irrigation Interval*			
	Summer		*Winter*	
	Light Soil	*Heavy Soil*	*Light Soil*	*Heavy Soil*
Up to 6 months	2-3 days	3-4 days	3-4 days	4-6 days
Above 6 months to 1.5 year	4-6 days	6-8 days	7-8 days	8-12 days
Above 1.5 year to 5 years	7-10 days	10-15 days	9-15 days	12-20 days

If it rains frequently, irrigation will be reduced accordingly. After flowering, it is recommended to provide irrigation 3-4 times at an interval of 15-20 days. It would result in increased production along with healthy, delicious and colorful fruit. An earthen ring has to be prepared around an adult tree where irrigation need to be provided, while for a young plant basin is required for irrigation water, so that less water is wasted.

At the base of the saplings, soil should be kept high so that rain water does not accumulate at the base or adequate drainage should be provided for rain water.

After one month of planting of saplings, it is recommended to **remove weeds present** in the garden by ploughing. It should also be done in old mango orchards during post harvest period.

To protect mango trees and its fruits from storm, it is advisable to plant 'storm stopping' trees e.g. *Debdaru, Kalojam, Jhau, Lambu, Sishu,* etc. trees in the southwestern side of the orchard. This is mainly on account of a stronger probability of south westerly storm in eastern part of the country during March April, a duration of flowering.

Extreme temperatures, both hot and cold, are harmful for the saplings. Temperature over 37.5^0 Celsius or below 7^0 Celsius causes immense damage to saplings aged 3-4 years. They can be protected from bad weather if covered by dry grass or straw.

After 1-2 years of planting the grafted sapling, they start flowering. It is suggested to break them off, because, it does not help the roots and branches to grow properly and the tree becomes very weak. If any branch comes out from the stock of the tree it is better to prune them off immediately. Further, it may be ensured that the plant grows straight for at least 1 meter. It should not have more than 4-6 branches spread out evenly in all direction.

To get regular and good production, both urea and phosphate fertilizers can be applied in required proportion twice every year. There is a need to increase the quantity of fertilizer according to growth of the tree.

6.4 Application of Fertilizers

Fertilizer in the quantity (mentioned in Table 6.3) per plant per year can be applied by mixing with the soil in two doses, i.e. once after collection of fruit or before *monsoon* (June-July) and again when fruits begin to form, keeping a distance of 1 feet from the base of the tree.

Irrigation is a necessary supplement after this application.

Table 6.3: Applications of Fertilizers per Tree

Name of the fertilizers	*1st year*	*Growing rate of quantity per year*	*Quantity for mature (aged) tree (10 year)*
Compost-dung/compost leaves/courtyard manure	40 kg.	6 kg.	100 kg.
Mustard or neemkhol	2.5 kg.	-	-
Urea	-	150 gm.	1.5 kg.
Super phosphate	-	125 gm.	1.25 kg.
Murate of potash	-	125 gm.	1.25 kg.

6.5 Diseases and Pests Attack

A sapling is prone to the following diseases and pests attack at an early age.

Anthracrose—Mango trees are prone to fungal attack in areas with heavy rainfall, moisture and humidity. It is seen in young leaves and branches. Initially, deep brown or black spot appears. Therefore, the young branches gradually dry up from the top. There is a need to keep the garden clean. It is essential to cut the affected part of the tree and burn it. In addition to this, Copper Oxichloride, e.g., Blitox @ 4 gms./lt should be mixed with water and sprayed. Further, Mancozeb, e.g., Dythen M 45 @ 2.5 gms./lt, Captan or Caftaf @2.0 gms/lt, Bavistin 1 gm/lt should be mixed with water and sprayed twice at an interval of 15 days. It is advisable to spray medicine in affected gardens in August-September.

Leaf-cutter Bug —In the beginning of monsoon a brown colored female pest lays eggs in the center of leaves and cuts the leaf in such a manner as if it has been cut off by a scissors. The affected leaves with egg drop to the ground. Many a time it is seen that most of the newly sprouted leaves of the affected branch are cut, resulting in the sapling becoming weak, which is detrimental to its normal growth. This problem is seen during monsoon only. Growing trees are also prone to such attack. Therefore, in order to get rid of these pests, during winter season, the orchard should be freed of weeds and the soil should be dug and mud loosened. When this type of attack is observed, Endosulphar (2 ml/lt) or Carboryl (2 g/lt) may be sprayed on the sprouting leaves. The affected leaves on the ground may be collected either for burning with the help of kerosene oil or for dumping them by pesticides to prevent further contamination.

Hole driller Bug—The larva of this pest makes a hole at the tip of growing branches and enters them. This hole could be as deep as 8-10 cm. As a result, the branches dry up. Spraying of Carboryl @ 3g/It water is recommended on new sprouting branches for good result. Injecting these holes with kerosene or petrol also gives good results.

Mealy Bug—The flat white colored pests are found on the branches sticking together. It looks as if a layer of curd has been applied on the branch. They suck the juice from the branch, resulting in the soft branches getting dried up. Diemithoete @1ml/lt water is recommended for spraying. During the month of November, it is advisable, to protect the tree from attack of these pests by covering the main trunk with a layer of mud and then by a polythene sheet of 1 foot width. Folidol powder can also be sprinkled around the main trunk.

6.6 Inter Cropping

As mango trees take longer time to yield profit to the grower, it is desirable to supplement one's income by growing some short-term crops till the orchard is not shaded by trees. Such crops when taken in the orchard are called inter crops. There is another kind of cropping in the orchard when the orchard soil is covered with some crop which in due course is turned back to the soil to supplement organic matter of the orchard soil. This is called cover crops. These two types of crops (inter crops and cover crops) are important operations in the management of a good orchard, although many growers do not pay much attention to it.

In case of traditional mango varieties, no fruits can be expected from mango trees during the initial 7-8 years. When the saplings are small, there is enough vacant-space in between the trees in the garden, the farmers can use the in-between space commercially. Some of the tips are illustrated hereunder:

Inter crops such as vegetables, legumes, short duration and dwarf fruit crops like chilly, ladies finger, brinjal, etc. can be cultivated during *kharif* season. During *rabi*, vegetables and pulses can be grown. During April, lady's finger, *moogdal*, soyabean can be cultivated. Fruits like papaya, guava, pineapple etc. can be grown depending on the agro-climatic condition of the region. The water and nutrient requirements of the inter crops must be met separately.

It is recommended not to grow turmeric, ginger or any crop which draw more nutrients from the soil. However, once the saplings grow into big trees, coriander, pulses etc. can be planted in between the trees where sunlight is available. It helps to safeguard soil erosion, enhance water retaining capacity and fertility.

Nowadays, cultivation of some flowers like marigold, *sarpagandha, aswagandha*, etc. is quite profitable.

Vegetables that have their roots within 25 cm depth of the soil are considered good for intercropping. These are tomato, beans, radish, *palak* etc. These vegetables can be taken profitably in a growing orchard by appropriate application of nutrients to the soil and also maintaining an optimum level of moisture. Among the annual crops, due consideration should be given to the legumes such as pea, lentil, moth bean, black gram and green gram.

While taking some of the short-term and early fruit bearing crops as an inter crop, due consideration is essential for the selection of a particular fruit. This is essential because the roots of such trees may start competing with the roots of main fruit trees for nutrient and moisture. The feeler trees, unless removed at appropriate time when primary fruit trees start giving economic crop, may create problems of low orchard efficiency. Keeping this point in mind, it is apparent that wherever pineapple and strawberry can be grown, these serve as ideal inter crops.

Wherever frost hazard is less, an inter crop like papaya can be taken profitably in a mango orchard. Likewise, in the northern plains of India, *'Sharbati* peach can be an excellent inter crop for mango orchard. *Phalsa* and guava can also be included in the early stage of growth of the trees, provided these are maintained properly by adequate pruning and removal at proper time.

The method of growing inter crop in an orchard is different in the young and the bearing orchards. In the former the entire land is utilized, leaving only the basin portion of the tree. The tree is located in the middle of the bed in which the crop is grown. As the trees grow in age, the size of the basin increases and the area of inter crops get reduced gradually. When the trees attain good bearing age, the inter crop is grown in between the tree rows in one direction, i.e. on two opposite sides of the trees, leaving the other two sides open. The trees are enclosed by a strong bund on two sides running from one end of the orchard to the other. This facilitates irrigation of the trees within the bonded space independent of the inter crop. It also provides space for movement during plant protection and other operation in the orchard.

While taking inter crop, a common mistake is committed. The fruit trees are left to obtain nutrients from the same fertilizer dose applied to the inter crops. This is one of the main causes of decline in mango production. The inter crop and the fruit trees must receive separately their independent requirements of fertilizer, irrigation and sunlight.

Besides, intercropping in orchard promotes infestation of pests and diseases in greater intensity than under clean cultivation. This is due to increase in the humidity and vegetation around the trees due to inter crops. Hence, regular plant-protection measures against pests and disease of the mango crop are essential. In case of mature mango orchard, inter crops can be grown where there is sufficient sunlight.

6.7 Principles of Inter Cropping

Inter crops should occupy a secondary place in the orchard, primary consideration being given to the orchard. Therefore, some principles are followed in inter cropping. The crops that may grow tall and have a tendency towards excessive growth should be discouraged. At least 120 cm radius must be left from the base of the growing fruit trees for taking inter crops. Such inter crops should be selected that do not exhaust the nutrients and moisture from the soil, essential for the growth of fruit trees. Perennial or exhaustive crops should be discouraged as an inter crop in the orchard. Bee farming in mango orchards gives scope for extra income and extra fruit production every year.

Inter cropping is practiced in both the districts of west Bengal but not extensively. Mostly brinjal, potato, *haldi*, *musur,* black *jeera* and dhania, *kalai dal,* elephant food, white potato is cultivated. In the old mango orchards consisting of the adult trees with big canopy, intercropping cannot be practiced due to lack of sunlight. The crops thus cultivated are sold to the market and they can earn Rs.24000/- to Rs.30,000/- per acre annually. One of the features observed in Malda district is that the open area with sunlight in the mango orchard is given to *bargadars* for cultivation of inter crops. He may be given financial assistance by the orchard owner. He will use his own labor and in turn give half the share of the vegetables produced to the owner. This is known as *'tal barga'*.

6.8 Cover Crops

These crops save the orchard soil from being eroded during the rainy season, particularly in areas where drainage is not proper. Water-holding capacity of the soil is increased and the biological complex of the soil is also improved. It is preferable to take leguminous crops for cover cropping so that nitrogen fixation in the orchard soil is facilitated. Another advantage of cover crops is that they will prevent the growth of weeds. During rainy season *(Kharif)* green gram, black gram, cow pea and *guar* are preferable. During winter season *(Rabi)*, it is desirable to take sweet clover (*Senji*), pea, lentil, moth bean and fenugreek. The most important point in the selection of cover crops is the requirement of water of a particular crop. If a particular crop needs to be irrigated very frequently when the orchard trees do not need water, this will certainly tell upon the productivity of the fruit trees. For example, if berseem is taken in a mango orchard during winter when fruit bud differentiation and flowering is expected and the orchard is irrigated too frequently, it may not be conducive to the productivity of the tree in general.

6.9 Cultural Schedule and its Importance -- Some Important Suggestions

Factors responsible for the decline of fruit yield and proper fruiting pattern mostly pertain to management practices such as nutrition of trees and control of weeds, insect pests and diseases. If the trees do not present a healthy appearance and leaves look somewhat yellowish, it is obvious that such trees suffer from under-nutrition.

If the cover crops or inter crops are taken regularly, the weeds will be automatically suppressed. A constant watch over the diseases and pests of mango is necessary for ensuring quality crop from trees. When the humidity builds up appreciably during the flowering time, incidence of mango hopper and powdery mildew is very much increased, and sometimes this may result in no fruit set.

One of the important schedules in mango orchard management is maintenance of excellent sanitary conditions in the orchard and regular pruning of the malformed parts (both vegetative and floral) in the tree, if any. This will ensure reduced incidence of mango malformation.

Proper irrigation of trees, particularly during summer, is very essential to get quality crop from the bearing trees and proper growth in young plants. While bearing trees ought to be irrigated at an interval of a fortnight during summer, younger plants need weekly irrigation.

Trees must be regularly observed for any setback due to any cause and steps must be taken immediately to remedy it. A proper round-the-year cultural schedule must be drawn up before hand and operations should be done as per schedule. This will ensure production of quality crop from healthy mango trees.

6.10 Irregular Bearing Habit of Mango Tree

Generally, mango trees do not bear fruit every year. It

is observed that a tree, which bears good number of fruits in a year, does not bear fruit or bears very few fruits in the subsequent year. This nature of mango trees is called irregular bearing. It is a serious problem and therefore in order to regularize the mango production the following steps can be taken.

It has been observed that two to three times evening-out of the land, regulated application of fertilizer and irrigation results in growth of new branches when the flower comes. These branches bear fruit during next winter. This method gives some production even in unproductive years.

To get flowers in extremely fast growing trees, it is advisable to remove 1 inch skin in a ring form from the branches of the tree. It must be done during August-September, i.e. before four months the flowering season. It results in increased content of carbohydrate and nitrogen in the branch which helps flowering.

It has been observed through various experiments that if in a particular tree in a particular year, flowers come in good quantity, it is better to destroy some. This helps in preserving nutrients in these branches which in turn help in growth of new leaves in these branches during summer and spring. It also helps flowering in these branches during the next season and regulating the irregular fruit bearing habit of the tree.

Some varieties bear fruits two to three times in a year. Generally ripe mangos of these varieties are not good in quality. But some are very good viz. *'chini dofola', topa dofola'*. These types can be grown to get production throughout the year.

Flowering of the trees is dependent on hormones present in the tree, like oxin, jibbareline or growth control hormone present in the tree. Good results are obtained when these hormones are externally sprayed.

Diseases and pest attack results in the loss of flower and reduce the volume of production. There is a need for spraying of medicine in appropriate quantity and on time help to control diseases and pests.

Mango trees respond well to organic manure applications. Organic manures such as vermicompost, *panchagavya* and vermiwash are used for promoting healthy growth and fruit formation. From the initial planting stages to caring of full grown trees, *Panchagavya* and vermicompost can be effectively used to supply essential nutrients to the trees and prevent pest infections. Vermicompost is prepared by using earthworms. Vermiwash is the liquid collected after the passage of water through a column of activated earthworms. It is very useful as an organic spray for all crops. *Panchagavya* is an organic growth promoter, which is prepared by mixing cow dung, cow urine, cow milk, curd and *ghee* in suitable proportions, and is sprayed on the plants. It contains several macro, micro nutrients, beneficial bacteria and fungi, which aid in growth promotion and act as effective pest repellents. It can be prepared by thoroughly mixing five kilos of fresh cow dung and one litre of cow's *ghee* in a plastic or cement tank or earthen pot. The mixture is stirred daily for three to four days. About three litres of cow's milk, two litres of cow's curd, three litres of sugarcane juice, three litres of tender coconut water and 10 to 12 bananas are mixed well and added to the mixture. The entire concoction is allowed to ferment for fifteen days. The container should be covered with a net (or) cotton cloth to allow aeration of the fermenting unit. The concoction is stirred two or three times a day for about fifteen days and then used. For mango trees of about 6-7 years age, vermicompost may be applied at the rate of 10 kilograms per tree in one litre of water may be sprayed over the foliage (crown) and at the base of the tree. Spraying *Panchagavya* over the crown and at the base of the tree must be done four to five times. The first spraying must be done before the flowering season (January-March) to increase flower formation. A second spraying must be done after 15-20 days. The process must be repeated till the flowers turn into small size buds. Once the buds start forming then the application can be done once a month. Use of Panchagavya and vermicompost has been found to increase the size, number and enhance the color of the fruits. The fruits thus grown become more acceptable for export.

6.12 Recommended Practices

The recommended practice for one hectare of mango tree is about 25 litres of *Pachagavya* (mixed in 750-800 litres of water) and four to five MT of vermicompost. Spraying *Panchagavya* has been found effective in the control of fruit fly menace, a common infection in all fruit bearing trees. Trees treated with organic manures bore large sized leaves and form a dense canopy with profuse rooting systems. The taste and shelf life of the fruits are also found to be more satisfactory. The interaction of the root hairs of these trees with the organic manures also increases the activity of the nitrogen-fixing bacteria in the soil. The organic manures also act as a carrier medium for the development of several beneficial micro organisms such as azospirillum, azotobacter, rhizobium and phosphor bacteria.

It was observed that in both the districts, some of the progressive orchard owners who are cultivating mangoes themselves have started using organic fertilizers and pest repellent. It was reported that it not only improves the health of the trees but also the quality and taste of the mangoes. These types of mangoes have high demand in the western countries and it is expected that as more and more farmers take up this practice, the export of mangoes will increase in the coming years. The District

Horticulture Department has taken initiative in explaining and motivating the farmers regarding this type of cultivation and Demonstration Camp.

6.13 Harvesting

The ripening and quality of a mango depends at what stage of maturity it is plucked. Premature plucking will affect the actual taste, smell and shape. Factors which help determine plucking of mango at the right time are-

- When yellow color appears on top of the fruit.
- When ripe mango starts dropping from tree.
- When the gravitational pull of the mango is between 1:1.01 and 1: 1.02, e.g., If a mango sinks in a bucket of water, then it is at the right stage of maturity.
- When there are 30 ripe mangoes out of 100 in the tree.

If the fruits are collected through the process of checking the branches, it may fall on the ground causing both external and internal damage to the fruit. The mango can be preserved for long if the fruit is collected with at least 8-10 mm. of its stalk. For this, proper apparatus should be used for safe collection of fruit. Mango collecting apparatus have a knife and a net at the head of a long bamboo pole. Mangoes are cut with a portion of stalk and brought down in the net. Collected mangoes are to be placed on a net made from bamboo in upside downslide so that the gum runs off and does not fall on the fruit. As a result, no black spot appear on the fruit and it can be preserved for a long time.

After collecting the fruit, it is necessary to sort immediately according to size and shape. Wooden boxes or card board boxes with a capacity of 50-100 mangoes are mostly used for packaging. The boxes should have sufficient number of holes to allow ventilation. To prevent any sort of damage, each fruit should be wrapped in newspaper and placed in the box.

Generally green mangoes plucked at maturity could be preserved for a longer time than ripe ones plucked from the tree. Regulated humidity, low temperature and usage of chemicals delay ripening of the mangoes. 5^0 - 10^0 c temperature and 85 - 90 per cent of relative humidity is ideal for storage of various varieties of mangoes. Very low temperature can damage mangoes. Paraffin layer (3%) on the mango gives it a longer shelf life. It can be preserved for two weeks if it is put into cold water of 12^0-15^0 c and with room temperature of 15^0C.

7

Marketing Aspects: Role of Different Channels, Market Arrivals and Price Spread

The healthy marketing system for a particular commodity has to provide required information, technology, marketing linkages for better price realization by farmers. Marketing efficiency of a particular commodity is evaluated by looking at the producer's share in the consumer's rupee. The present chapter addresses the issues effecting marketing of mango.

7.1 A. Andhra Pradesh

The major commercial varieties of mango marketed in Andhra Pradesh are Banganapalli, Neelam, Tota Purii, Subarna Rekha.

Marketing Channels for Mango —-Based on the discussion with the farmers, traders and representatives of processing units, it was observed that mango reaches to the consumers through four channels, i.e,

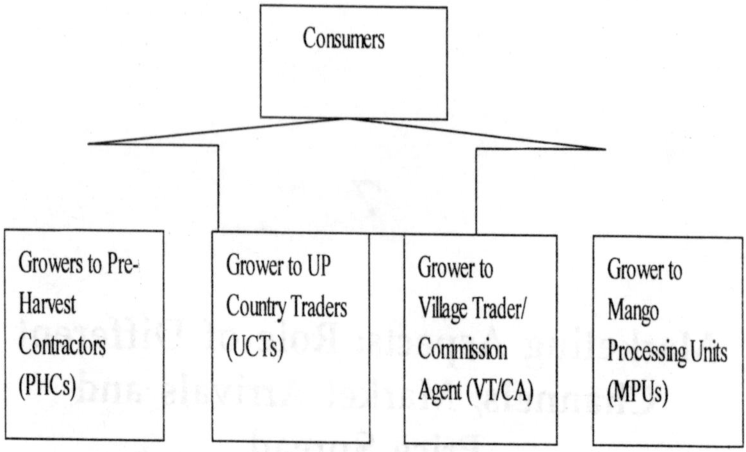

Chart 7.1: Marketing Channel of Mango

From the grower, mango reaches the export destination through any of these four channels. A comprehensive chart depicting different channels/ sub-channels is depicted below:

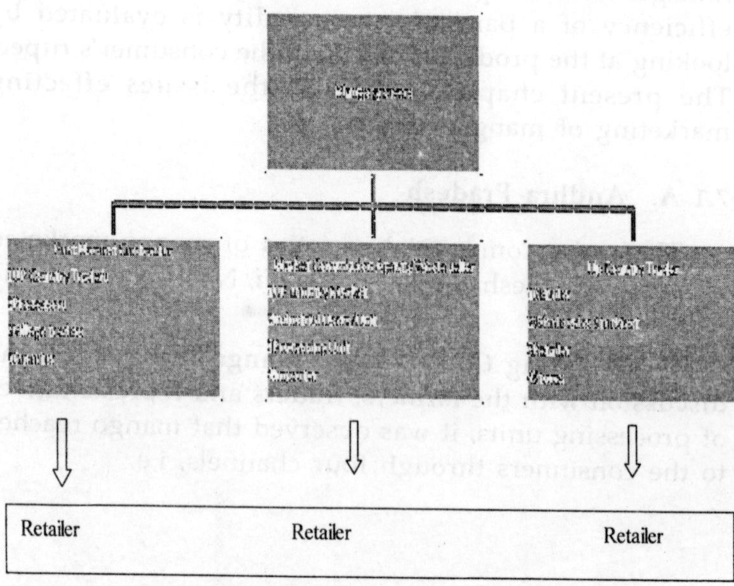

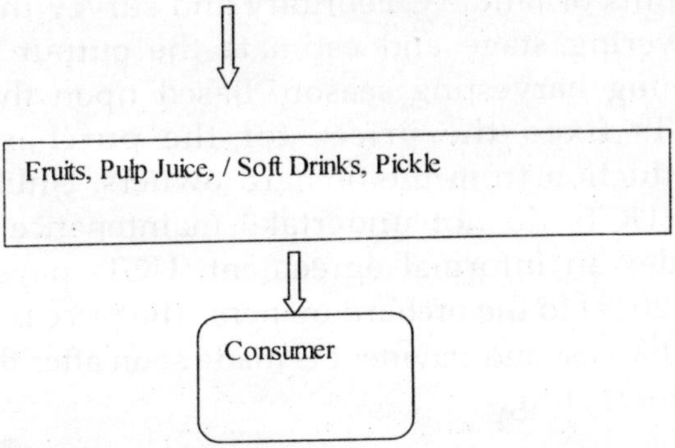

Chart 7.2: Export Destination of Mango –Different Channels and Sub Channels

7.2. Pre-harvest Contractor (PHC)

The orchard owner leases out his orchard as per contract to the PHCs. Both the parties agree to abide by the terms and conditions stipulated at the time of agreement (which is almost invariably oral in nature). The PHCs visit the mango orchards just after the mango harvesting season (during August/ September) to survey the orchards. On completion of the survey, the negotiation takes place between the grower and contractor. These contractors also take up the works of required input application to the leased in orchards including plant protection to obtain optimum fruit yield. PHCs after harvesting mango sell it in the open market or to processing units like a grower who under takes self-marketing.

7.3. Up Country Traders (UCTs)

Many traders from neighbouring states visit mango markets in Chittor and Krishna districts during mango season. Traders from Bangalore, Chennai, Mumbai, New Delhi, Kolkata, Nagpur, Jaipur, Ahmedabad and Hyderabad participate in mango trading in Chittor and Krishna districts. UCTs visit mango orchards during the months of January, February and survey the orchards at flowering stage and estimate the output for the forth coming harvesting season. Based upon the estimation, UCTs fixed the prices for the purchase of mango production from the orchard owners. Unlike the PHCs, the UCTs do not undertake maintenance of the farm. Under an informal agreement, UCTs pays an advance (10-20 %) to the orchard owners. The price is settled before the harvest and payment is made soon after the completion of marketing.

7.4. Mango Processing Units

The mango processing activity in Chittor district commenced during 1965 with enterprising fruit merchants, M/S Haneef and Sattar, setting up a small unit named HANSTAR, at Damalcheru to extract mango pulp which worked for few years only (Naidu, 2002). A more organized was to words the growth of the cluster was initiated by the prominent mango grower Late Subramanya Reddy who established M/S India Canning Industries, the first merchandised fruit processing unit. However, no new units were commissioned during the period 1971-80. Thereafter mango pulp units were formed at a frequent interval.

The processors purchase mango for production of pulp from traders as well as mango growers. Totapuri mangoes are mainly used for preparing pulp because of its pulp-yielding rate. The processors reach the mango orchards, testify the quality, determine the price and offer advances to the growers. As the pulp content depends upon the quality, processors insist on sorting and grading of mangoes and prices are determined accordingly. Processing units purchase mangoes from market yards as they are assured of large quantities to run the unit continuously till the mango season is over.

7.5. Village Trader (VT)/Commission Agent (CA)

About 60 per cent of mango growers transact through village trader/commission agent (VT/CA). VTs often provide advance to the farmer with the condition that grower has to sell his produce to them. They resell mangoes to UCTs/retailers. But VT collects 10 per cent of volume of trade amount towards commission charges. If due to any unforeseen situation (Pests, cyclones etc) the growers fail to settle the advance, the same gets adjusted from the next year sale proceeds. However, inadequate information of prices and lack of weighting facilities are a few limitations of these channels,

Over all, mango reaches to the consumers through five different channels (Table 7.1). However, it is very difficult to come out with a clear cut demarcation of channels as some PHCs also act as CAs, some CAs act as traders. They themselves also act as local whole sellers. Many of the CAs / traders are also mango orchard owners and contribute substantially to the mango production. Discussions with the different players in the market as mentioned above revealed the following types of marketing channels.

Table 7.1: Share of Different Marketing Channels of Fresh Mangoes in Andhra Pradesh

S.No.	Marketing Channels	Share (%)
1.	Grower— —CAs/VTs—UCTs— —Retailers— —Consumer	55.0
2.	Grower —PHCs — CAs— —Retailer— —Consumer	25.0
3.	Grower— —UCTs— —Retailers— —Consumers	10.0
4.	Grower—Local Wholesalers —Retailer—Consumer	7.0
5.	Grower— —Processors	3.0
6.	Growers— — —Consumer	Negl
	Total	100.0

7.6. Mango Market Yards in Chittor and Krrishna Districts

Mango production in Chittor district arrives to five different market yards. They are Chittor, Damancheruvu, Bangarupalem, Tirupatti, and Puttur. In Krishna district mango production mostly arrives to Nunna MY in Vijayawada. In Chittor market yard varieties of mango arrive. The commission agents facilitate the trade between the mango farmers and purchasers. Putur market yard handles smaller quantities of mango. As it lies on the Tirupathti-Chennai Highway, mango production reaches either Tirupati or Chennai from the mango orchards directly. In Tirupati market yard, three varieties (Bangana Palli, Tota Puri, and Neelam) of mangoes are being traded. The arrivals of mangoes are mainly from outside the notified area such as Putur, Nagari, Kodur (Kapada district). Damalacheruvu market yard, one of the oldest private market yards in Chittor district, consists of about 100 mandies. It is an open market and no action takes place. Mangoes arrive from Vellore, Kuppam and all the mondals of the district. The traders from far off place like Delhi, Kolkata, Raipur, Ahmadabad, Nagpur, Mumbai, Bangalore, visit this market yard for buying mangoes. The command area of Bangarupalyam market yard covers four mandals. It covers 77 villages consisting of about 1000 mango growers. The arrivals of mangoes are from the command area.

The Nuna market yard under Golapudi AMC near Vijaywada consists of 81 shops. Every year about 7,000 to 8,000 trucks each containing 10-11 metric ton mangoes are being exported in different parts of the country mainly in Azadpur mandi of Delhi. Traders in this market yards also provide finance to the farmers. Major varieties of mango, ie Benishan, Totapuri etc are coming to Nunna MY. About 15 to 20 per cent of Totapuri mango comes to this market and the rest is sold in the orchard itself.

Maharashtra, Gujarat, and West Bengal use this for picking in the early season. About 70 per cent of mangoes are exported to other states and rest 30 per cent is sold to local traders. Traders from Maharashtra, Gujarat, West Bengal visit Nunna MY and take advantage of early season pickling, when the prices remain usually high.

7.7. Market Arrivals and Prices of Mango

The annual arrivals of mangoes and prices in five market yards in Chittor and Nunna market yard in Krishna districts during 1997-98 to 2005-06 is presented in **Annexure 21.**

The continuous drought conditions in Chittor district during the last four years had hampered the arrival of major agricultural produce in the market yard. Further, production of mango fluctuates due to alternate bearing nature of the crop, which affects the market arrival as well. Absence of effective marketing linkages also hampers the mango arrival to various market yards. Growers prefer to sell directly to processing units, local/ outside whole sellers.

Mango prices vary a great deal from year to year, depending upon each year's total production and various other factors like the prevailing prices, demand, transport, marketing facilities etc. Whole sale prices of mango also vary considerably based on the supply / demand of particular varieties, periods of availability, weather condition; variety quality etc. Daily arrivals have also a direct bearing on the prices. Thus, the fluctuations in prices are of an irregular pattern. Ordinarily, the prices are high at the commencement of the season. They start declining gradually as the supplies increase. Later on, when the arrivals decrease, they tend to recover and reach a high level again before the close of the season. The monthly whole sale price index of mangoes (All India) for ten years period is presented in **Annexure 22.**

7.8 Role of UP Country Traders in Price Fixation

The field study revealed that UCTs obtain supply prospects of mango from the village and supply to the terminal markets. UCTs acting as traders, also determine prices at the village level and at the terminal markets. In fact, daily price depends upon visit to number of UCTs in the village and market yard every day. If number of UCTs is large, mango price is reported to be high and vice versa. Thus, influence of UCTs is high on prices than the local traders. Mango growers' mostly small and marginal farmers are unaware of the final price of their produce, which they sell to the traders. Farmers feel cheated as traders garner higher margin.

However, as UCTs facilitate selling of mangoes on the farm itself, small farmers those who do not have their own transport are greatly benefited. If UCTs purchase from the market, UCTs engage in financial links with mandi owners (Traders). Traders borrow from UCTs before the mango season to meet working capital requirement and the account is settled in installments or at the season. After the purchase from the farmers or market depending upon the distance, transport arrangements are made by the UCT. Around 400 trucks take mango to UP country markets every day during the season (April-May) from Nuzivid mandal of Krishna district. About 40-45 rakes are exported in a year from this station (One rack= 40 wagons x 26 MT = 1040 MT).Similarly, about 100 trucks leave from Damancheruvu market yard in Chittor to different places in North India.

7.9. Role of Commission Agents

The commission agents (CAs) are the most important link in the marketing of mango controlling about two-thirds of the total markets. These CAs also act as grower cum trader and facilitate the trade between the mango grower and UCTs. The study revealed that the purchasers normally pay Rs 60 for loading/ unloading/grading of mangoes to CAs. They are required to pay 1 per cent of the turn over as market fee to the AMC and 4 per cent of the turnover as commission to the CAs. The CA collects the market fee from purchasers on behalf of the AMC. For this purpose the AMC provides receipts to the CAs. CAs, who are also traders, avail Secured Over Draft (SOD) from banks and utilize the same in lending to mango farmers for consumption/ production purpose { @24 per cent interest per annum }.The amount of advance is decided on several factors such as areas under mango, expected production, past track record of the mango supply to the CAs etc. After harvest of mangoes, farmers sell mangoes to the CAs and 10 per cent of the sale proceeds as commission charges.

7.10. Price Spread

Price spread is the difference between the retail price paid by the consumer and the price received by the farmer/ producer for same quantity of the produce. Price spread in marketing of mango is analyzed by following the product movement in from the mango grower to the consumer. Various costs (particularly marketing costs) and margins together with the farm gate price constitute the consumer price of mango. It is a fact that there is a direct relationship between the consumer price and the length of the marketing channel. In other words, the consumer price is the lowest when marketing is the shortest, ie when the mango grower directly sells to the consumers. However, the magnitude of sale takes place through the direct channel was negligible. In the absence of direct linkage between mango grower and the consumer, it is the middle men alone who have been taking the advantage of the situation. An indicator of the efficiency of any supply chain is the extent of price spread between producer and consumer. A high price spread would indicate a lower efficiency. Conversely, a low level of price spread would denote a high efficiency of the supply chain mechanism. Producer's share in the consumer price is high when the marketing efficiency is high. The **price spread** in different channels of mango marketing is presented in **Annexure 23**.

The marketing margin as percentage of consumer minus producer price difference is a measure of efficiency of the marketing channel. High per cent indicates low efficiency and vice versa. The Producer's share in consumer price and market margins as percentage of consumer minus producer price differentials in various channels of marketing of mangoes is furnished in table below:.-

Table 7.2: Producer's Share in Consumer's Price and Marketing Efficiency in Andhra Pradesh

No. Marketing Channels	*Producer's share in Consumer Price*	*Margin as % of consumer-producer price differential*	*Market Efficiency*
1. Grower–CAs/VTs–UCTs–Retailer–Consumer	28.80	63.80	High
2. Grower –PHCs –CAs–Retailers–Consumers	34.74	68.50	Lowest
3. Grower–UCTs–Retailers–Consumers	33.59	65.50	Low
4. Grower–Wholesalers–Retailers–Consumers	44.05	62.20	Higher
5. Grower– –Consumer	100.00	0.00	Highest

Source: Field data.

B. Maharashtra

7.11. Marketing Channels for Alphonso Mango

The majority of farmers of Sindhudurg send their mangoes

through transporter to the **commission agents** at Vashi and Pune, who market on behalf of the farmers. The sale price, total amount payable, and various deductions like transportation charges, commission (8 % in Pune and 10% in Vashi), loading and unloading (up to 5 per cent) are immediately conveyed to the farmers through a receipt known as **Patti.** Some commission agents used to deduct the postage charges for forwarding the patti to the farmers.

A few farmers, who are not tied up with commission agents, send their mangoes to other markets where prices are higher. A few enterprising farmers were directly selling a part of their produces through their contact at Mumbai, Nasik and Pune. These channels fetched maximum price to the farmers. Local sales from the orchards were limited from the left out mangoes, which are sold directly to the processors towards the end of June. The average sale pattern through the channels for the sample farms during 2005-06 is indicated in the Table7.3 below:

Table 7.3: Channel of Mango Marketing in Maharashtra during 2005-06

Channels	*Number of farmers*	*Portion of Produce*	*Average Price (kg/ha)*
Farmer—Commission Agents—Wholesaler ——Retailer—Consumer-	25	90%	30
Farmer—Consumer	02	01%	35
Farmer—Processor	12	05%	12

Source: Field Data.

7.12. Marketing Cost and Average Price Realized by Farmers

An attempt has been made to examine the share of mango farmers in the price paid by the consumer. Details are depicted in table below.

Table 7.4: Cost Incurred and Price Realized by Alphonso Mango in Maharashtra

Particulars	*Age of Orchard (Years)* Less than 15	15-25	Above 25	*Weighted average of Samples*
Total No of Fruit Bearing Trees with the Farmers	916	347.3	682.5	595
Annual Maintenance Cost per Tree in Rs	573.4	658.2	624.1	628
Cost of Marketing per Tree in Rs	757.8	813.1	835.8	811
Grand Total of Annual Cost per Tree	1331.2	1471.3	1459.9	1439
Average Yield per Tree in Kg	77.2	79.9	82.2	80
Average Cost per Kg	17.4	18.4	17.7	18
Weighted Average Price Realized per Kg	30.2	30.2	29.1	30
Weighted Average of per Kg Share of Farmers in the Sale Price	**12.8**	**11.7**	**11.5**	**12**

Source: Field Data.

The weighted average cost of maintenance and marketing of the produce of a tree come to Rs 357 and Rs 507 respectively. The mango grower realizes a minimal surplus of Rs 12 per kg. This is primarily because of the unusually high expenditure incurred in marketing of the produce. The expenditure incurred for production and marketing of one kg of Alphanso mango and percentage share ot each item of expenditure are shown in Table 7.5.

Table 7.5: Marketing Expenses and their Share in the Price of One Kg of Alphonso

Factors of Production	*PC&L*	*CP &L*	*Transp.*	*Com,&H*	*SPR*	*FS*
Amount (Rs) in price of 1 kg	7.85	2.95	3.13	4.07	30	12
Percent share in price of 1 kg	**26.17**	**9.83**	**10.43**	**13.57**	**-**	**40**

Source: Field Data, Note— PC&L= Production Cost and Labor, CP&L= Cost of Petti and Labor, Com& H= Commission and Hamali, SPR= Sale Price Realized, and FS=Farmer's Surplus

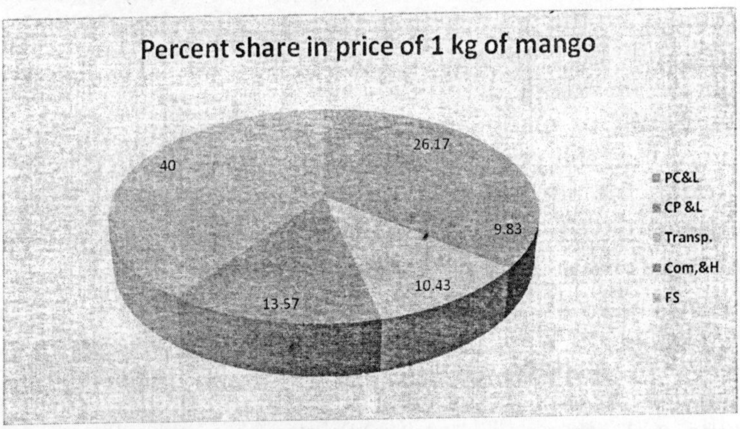

Graphic 7.1: Per cent Share of 1 kg of Mango.

The above data reveals that the marketing expenditure is considerably more than the annual maintenance cost of tree. There is hardly any scope for reduction in cost under 'Production Cost' and 'Cost of Peti', 'Packing Charges' etc. In view of the fact that Alphanso mango needs to be marketed at distance places, existing packaging process is most suitable and cost effective. However, if the mangoes are marked locally, the cost on packaging can be substantially reduced. Further, the transportation cost can be minimized by opening marketing centers in the locality/district head quarters. Similarly, the cost towards 'Commission, and Hamali" etc., which accounts for 13.57 per cent of price realized in sale of 1 kg of Alphanso mango, can also be reduced if the produce is marketed locally, as commission, as high as 10 per cent is being charged by Commission Agents in urban marketing centers of APMC, Vashi. Therefore, provision of marketing outlets locally is pertinent in order to increase the share of the primary grower in the ultimate price paid by the consumers.

7.13. Role of Transport Operators (TOs) and Commission Agents (CAs) in Marketing

The commissions Agents (CA) cum Wholesalers (WS) normally lift the produce from the mango growers through local transport operator. The wholesalers (WSs) also operate in the field through sub agents. On receiving the 'Pettis' of mango from the mango grower, the CA determines the per Petti price through open Auction or through the nontransparent *rumali system*. On the basis of the price so determined, the *CAs* issue patties to the grower. A Patti indicates the amount payable to the farmer with details such as cost of the mangoes and deduction towards transportation. Agent's commission, Hamali (Mazdoor) charges, octorai,*Tapal Charge* (Postage) etc. The commission was 10 per cent in vashi and 08 per cent in Pune and other markets during the period of study.

a. Transport Operators—A transport Agent at Vengurle, Sindhudurg is in the business of collecting mangoes and sending them to traders on a commission for the last forty years. During 2004-05, he had transported 1, 35,000 pettis (2025MT) to Mumbai and 30, 3000 pettis (450MT) to Belgaon. Similarly, during 2005-06, he had sent 1, 25,000 pettis (1875 MT) to Mumbai and 25,000 pettis (375MT) to Belgaon in Karnataka. The transporter normally, sends the pettis to Vashi market in truck loads. However, if the pettis collected are less than a truck load, the stock is sent by bus or train. The transportation charges during 2005-06 came to around Rs 5 per petti, which included truck charges of Rs 25-32 , labor charges for loading and unloading, and handling charges in the godown, toll charges and miscellaneous charges including administrative charges of the transporter. There are number of such transporter throughout the district.

b. Commission Agents (CAs)—The CA has their offices in mandis/ market places. In majority of the cases these agents arrange to transport mango pettis from the orchard to the market place .The CAs start paying advances to the mango growers in November and December to enable growers to carry out various farming operations. Such advance payments range between 10 and 30/40 per cent of anticipated value of production, which in turn is arrived at on the basis of average production of last 5-10 years. Some commission agents do not make advance payments as there is possibility that farmers might sell the produce in cash to an agent other than from advance is received. In most of the cases the CAs have developed cordial relation with the farmers over the years and take advantage of these trust to lift the produce on a continuous basis. The Agents often encash the relationship and make a little advance payments to win over the farmers. The advance paid to the farmers prior to the production is not adjusted against the sale price of mango at the time to final settlement of account (pattis) with the farmers in the month of June. The CA was not ready to reveal their margin. The strong linkages between marketing and credit (advance payments) are clearly visible in the study area. However, their relationship is weakening with increase of Kisan Credit Card (KCC) and awareness of the farmers about other markets as reported by some of the CAs and farmers.

7.14. Efficiency of Marketing Channels

Due to the presence of Commission Agents (CA) and

Wholesaler (WSs,) and retailers, the cost of production get multiplied and the burden is ultimately borne by the consumer, in the form of higher prices. Similarly, this increased expenditure on the items of marketing, other than production, also resulted in the reduction of producer's share in consumer's price. In table 7.5 the per cent share of expenditure in the price of 1 kg of mango paid by the consumer is 26.17 per cent under production cost, 9.83 per cent towards cost of packing, 10.43 per cent towards transportation and 13.57 per cent towards commission and hamali charges, thus leaving 40 per cent of the consumer price towards share of the farmers. It is entirely the producer's surplus as the cost of production is already taken into account. The percentage spread being 20, marketing efficiency is low. The marketing efficiency can be increased by reducing the interference on the commission agents, thereby lowering the intermediate cost.

7.15. Arrival and Prices of Kesar Mangoes in Aurangabad

The commission agents and traders charge commission for marketing the produce. There is no standard procedure for charging commission. However, in APMC markets, there are approved rate for charging commission by agents. Farmers were spending about Rs 3, on an average, for marketing one petti of Kesar mango in Aurangabad Market. Arrival and Prices of Kesar Mangoes in Aurangabad petti is presented in table below:—

Table 7.6: Arrivals and Prices of Kesar Mangoes in Aurangabad during 2004 to 2006

(Arrivals in ton and modal price in Rs per quintal)

Year/Month	*2004*		*2005*		*2006*	
	Arrivals	*Modal Price*	*Arrivals*	*Modal Price*	*Arrivals*	*Modal Price*
March	25.00	556.43	13.30	1077.22	14.90	2193.33

April	174.50	603.42	65.40	819.74	55.70	2565.28
May	137.10	673.68	86.80	653.41	182.20	1607.89
June	129.00	650.00	141.10	591.35	180.00	1017.0
A.A.P@	—	634.49	—	678.71	—	1505.72

Source: Field Data, @ AAP= Average annual price

It is observed from table above that there is substantial increase in the modal prices during 2006. Modal price is the price in a distribution that occurs most frequently.

7.16. Marketing Cost and Average Price Realized by Farmers in Kesar Mango in Aurangabad

Weighted average costs for annual maintenance and marketing of the produce of a tree has been arrived at Rs 337 and Rs 495 respectively (table 7.7). The mango grower realizes a net income of Rs 13 per kg, which includes cost of own labor and supervision. The details of expenses incurred and income derived by the farmers are critically analyzed in the table below:—

Table 7.7: Cost Incurred and Price Realized by Kesar Mango in Aurangabad, Maharashtra

Particulars	*Age of Orchard (Years)*			*Weighted average*
	Less than 10	*10-15*	*Above 15*	*of Samples*
Total No of Fruit Bearing Trees with the Farmers	448.33	1505.83	1762.50	1089
Annual Maintenance Cost per Tree in Rs	298.50	631.83	378.00	337
Cost of Marketing per Tree in Rs	344.67	567.67	731.00	495
Grand total of Annual Cost per Tree (Rs)	643.17	929.50	1109.00	832
Average yield per Tree in Kg	48.67	71.67	85.00	64
Average cost per Kg in Rs	13.17	12.67	13.00	13

Weighted Average Price Realized per Kg in Rs	26.50	26.00	27.00	26
Weighted average of per Kg Share of Farmers in the Sale Price (%age)	**13.00**	**13.17**	**14.00**	**13**

Source: Field Data.

The expenditure towards annual maintenance in case of Kesar mango tree is less than that of Alphonso mango tree. The average annual maintenance for Kesar mango tree is Rs 337 as against Rs 628 for an Alphonso tree. Further, marketing cost in respect of Kesar mango at Rs 19 per peti of 2.5 kg ie. Rs 8 per kg is much less in comparison to that of Alphonso mango at Rs 162 per peti of 16 kg ie. Rs 10 per kg. However, due to variation in yield, the Kesar mango growers get the net surplus of Rs 13 per kg whereas the same in respect of Alphonso mango was Rs 12 per kg.

7.17. Marketing Expenses and their Share in the Price of One Kg of Alphonso Mango

The expenditure incurred for production and marketing of one kg of Kesar mango and percentage share of each item of expenditure are shown in Table 7.8:-

Table 7.8: Marketing Expenses and their Share in the Price of One Kg of Kesar Mango

Factors of Production	*PC&L*	*CP &L*	*Transp.*	*Com,&H*	*SPR*	*FS*
Amount (Rs) in price of 1 kg	5.27	4.66	1.77	1.30	26.00	13.00
Percent share in price of 1 kg	**20.27**	**17.93**	**6.81**	**5.00**	**-**	**50.00**

Source: Field Data, Note— PC&L+ Production Cost and Labor, CP&L= Cost of Peti and Labor, Com&H= Commission, Hamali etc, SPR= Sale price realized, and FS=Farmer's Surplus.

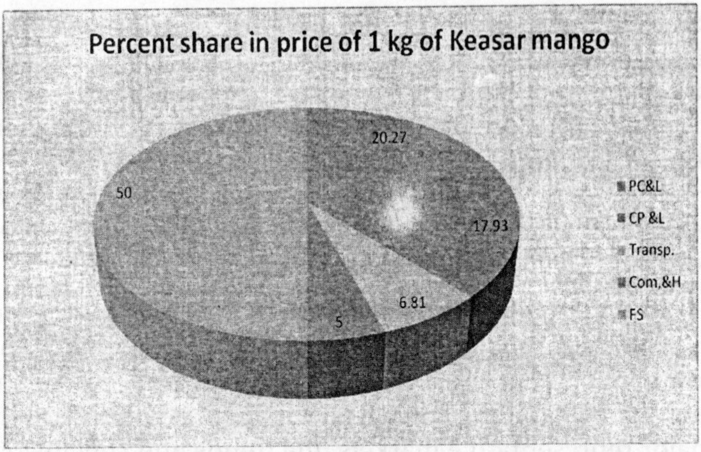

Graphic 7.2: Per cent Share of 1 kg of Kesar Mango

The above table indicates that marketing expenses is almost one and half times more than the annual maintenance cost of tree. There is hardly any scope for reduction under 'Production Cost' and 'Cost of Petti', 'Packing Charges' etc. However, the transport can be minimized by opening market centers in the locality or district head quarters. Therefore, provision of marketing outlets locally may increase the share of the primary grower in the ultimate sale price.

7.18. Relationship between Prices and Arrivals of Mango

The mango produced in the state is mainly marketed in urban centers ie Vashi, Pune, Nasik, Nagpur and Aurangabad. Besides, it is being marketed in Surat, Bangalore and Hyderabad. Mango in the state is mostly harvested and marketed during March to July. The trend in price of mango is simply reflective of its market arrivals, which in turn entirely depends on plucking of manufactured fruits from the trees as mango has a very short shelf life.

The correlation and regression analysis has been drawn to establish relationship between the prices of mango in some of the markets in Maharashtra and arrivals. This relationship was exiled for major markets of Aurangabad and Kolhapur for which reliable and comparable data are available on daily basis. Daily basis data were considered more relevant than aggregated weekly and monthly data. The daily data on peak season (March to May) are taken into account for the three years 2004, 2005 and 2006.

In Aurangabad, Kesar variety of mango is grown and in Kolahpur division mainly Alphonso is grown. This comparison also is based on the ground level prices and arrivals of Alphonso and Kesar mango. As these are the major representative markets, the trends and conclusions are more or less applicable to the rest of the markets of Maharashtra. The results are given in the table below:-

Table 7.9: Relationship between Prices and Arrivals of Mango in Maharashtra

Market	*Year*	*Period*	*CRC@*	*Constant (a)*	*P.C** (b)*	*DF #*	R^2
Aurangabad	2006	Mar-May	-0.5095	1755.68 (3.62)*	-0.61(-.14)*	49	0.26
	2005	Mar-May	-0.6308	860.52 (4.24)*	-0.69(-6.14)*	57	0.4
	2004	Mar-May	0.1578	156.24(0.31)	0.81(1.12)	49	0.02
Kolahpur	2006	Mar-May	-0.215	2148.35(0.98)	-0.47(-1.88)	73	0.05
	2005	Mar-Apr	-0.2196	1339.91(0.61)	-0.25(-0.87)	15	0.05
	2004	Mar-May	-0.5139	11185.75(3.98)*	-0.58(-3.00)*	25	0.26

Source: Prices and arrivals data from http//agmarknet.nic.in (cmmdatrep.asp), Note—figures in brackets are "t" values and * indicates significance at 99 % level, @ states correlation coefficient, **denotes price coefficient and # shows degree of freedom.

In case of Aurangabad market, the regression coefficient of price is negative and significant in 2005 and 2006 while it was positive but not significant in 2004. In Kolahpur market, the regression coefficient of price is negative in 2004, 2005 and 2006 though it was significant in 2004 only. Hence, these estimated equations largely substantiate the inverse relationship between arrivals and price. They move in the opposite direction. In the event of more arrival there is a fall in market price. During the study it was gathered that farmers try to disperse supply and realize higher prices in different markets.

C. West Bengal

7.19. Price

As stated earlier the wholesale price of mangoes in Malda, West Bengal varies considerably because of prevalence of various factors. There is no uniform pattern for price quotations. Thus the sale of mangoes, both in wholesale and retail trade, varies from place to place causing great confusion for comparing prices in different markets. However, attempt has been made to record the maximum and minimum price of different varieties of mango in Malda during 2004 to 06 **(Annexure 24).**

It revealed from the data in the Annexure that Amrapali fetched highest price at Rs 1500 per quintal followed by Himsagar at Rs 1,300 per quintal, Langra at Rs 1,200 per quintal and Laxman / Gopalbhog Rs 1,000 per quintal during 2004. Price realized for Amrapali mango, however, reduced to Rs 1,300 per quintal in 2005 and 2006. The same trend was noticed in other varieties also.

8

Economics of Mango Orchards

This chapter deals with farm economics of Mango Cultivation based on sample borrowers in selected districts like Chittor and Krishna of Andhra Pradesh; Sindhudurg and Aurangabad of Maharashtra; Malda and Murshidabad of West Bengal. It is important to examine the economic viability of the investment in order to assess its worthiness .The financial soundness of the investment is examined by analyzing the cash flows generated during the life of the investment. Internal rate of return (IRR) is worked out on the basis of present worth of cash earning.

8.1. Economics of Mango Orchards in Chittor and Krishna Districts, Andhra Pradesh

The economics mango orchard in selected districts of Andhra Pradesh is presented in Table below:-

Table 8.1: Yield, Cost of Investment, Cost of Maintenance and Net Income of Mango per Hectare in Andhra Pradssh

Particulars/ Age	*1-5*	*6-14*	*15-35*
1. Yield (MT/ ha)	0	6.5	12.5
2. Selling Price (Rs/MT)	0	4,500	4,500

3. Gross Income (Rs/ ha)	0	29,250	56,250
4. Cost of Investment/Capital Cost	62,500 (Rs/ha)	0	0
5. Cost of Maintenance (Rs/ ha)	0	13,750	13,750
6. Net Income (Rs/ha)	**-62,500**	**15,500**	**42,500**

Source: Field data.

Taking into account Chittor and Krishna districts together the average yield of mango stood at 6.5 metric ton per hectare in the age group of 6 to 14 years, while the stabilized yield recorded at 12.5 metric ton per hectare for orchards having attained the age bracket of 15 to 35years. Annual gross income worked out to Rs 29,500 per hectare and Rs 56,500 per hectare in the lower and higher age groups respectively. The net income earned were Rs15, 500 per hectare and 42,500 per hectare in the same age groups. The entire capital cost would be covered in four years, if the borrowers resort to own fund. Otherwise the amount would be capitalized in the event of institutional finance.

8.2 Maharashtra—Sindhudurg (Alphonso)

Attempt has been made to assess annual net income accrued per hectare in Alphonso and Kesar varieties of mango in Sindhudurg and Aurangabad districts respectively (Tables 8.2 and 8.3).

Table 8.2: Yield, Cost of Investment, and Cost of Maintenance and Net Income of Alphonso variety of Mango per hectare in Sindhudurg of Maharashtra

Particulars/ Age	*1-5*	*6-14*	*15-35*
1. Yield (MT/ ha)	0	4.52	4.73
2. Selling Price (Rs/MT)	0	30,000	29,200
3. Gross Income (Rs/ ha)	0	1,35,600	1,37,643
4 Capital Cost (Rs/ha)	1,84,996	0	0

5. Cost of Maintenance (Rs/ha)	0	35,401	35,886
6. Cost of Marketing	0	45,116	48,059
7. Total Cost (4+5+6)	1,84,996	80,575	83,945
6. Net Income (Rs/ha)	**-1,84,996**	**55,024**	**53,698**

Source: Field data.

8.3. Maharashtra—Aurangabad

Table 8.3: Yield, Cost of Investment, Cost of Maintenance and Net Income of Kesar Variety of Mango in Aurangabad per Hectare

Particulars/ Age	*1-5*	*6-14*	*15-35*
1. Yield (MT/ ha)	0	3.46	4.88
2. Selling Price (Rs/MT)	0	26,000	27,000
3. Gross Income (Rs/ ha)	0	89,960	1,31,760
4. Capital Cost (Rs/ha)	1,36,244	0	0
5. Cost of Maintenance (Rs/ ha)	0	18,996	21,735
6. Cost of Marketing	0	26,229	42,033
7. Total Cost(4+5+6)	1,36,244	45,225	63,767
6. Net Income (Rs/ha) {3-7}	**-1,36,244**	**44,773**	**67,993**

Source: Field data.

Average yield of Alphonso mango was higher than Kesar. It was 4.5 MT/ha compared to 3.46 Mt / ha during 6 to 14 years. However, the stabilized yield of Alphanso mango during 15 to 35 was lower at 4.73 MT/ ha as against Kesar mango 4 .88 MT/ ha). The annual net income earned per hectare was higher (Rs 55,024 /ha) in Alphanso mango than Kesar mango (Rs 44,773 /ha) during tender age. During adult period kesar mango earned higher net income at Rs 67,993/ha) compared to Alphanso mango (Rs 53,698/ha).

8.4. Malda of West Bengal

The fazli variety of mango earned maximum net income to the level of Rs 1,06,340 per hectare followed by Aswina at Rs 78,000 per hectare, Langra (Re 28,150/ha) and Himsagar (Rs 18,750/ha).

8.5 Cost and Revenue per hectare of Model Orchard (50 Tree) in Malda

Cost and revenue per hectare of Model Orchard (50 tree) is given below

Table 8.4: Cost and Revenue per hectare –Model Orchard of Unique Variety (50 Trees /ha) in Malda, West Bengal

Variety	*PT(Qtl)*	*TP(Qtl/ha)*	*FGP (Rs/Qtl)*	*TCO(Rs/ha)*	*R(Rs/ha)*	*NI(Rs/ha)*
1.Aswina	8	400	725	30,000	2,90,000	74,000
2.Fazli	9	450	725	30,000	3,26,250,	2,96,000
3.Langra	7	350	890	30,000	3,11,500	2,81,500
4.Himsagar	5	300	725	30,000	2,17,500	1,87,500
5.Laxmanbhog	5	250	600	30,000	1,50,000	1,20,000
6.Gopalbhog	5	250	550	30,000	1,37,500	1,07,500

Source:—Field data, Note—PT= Production/Tree, TP=Total Production, FGP=Farm Gate Price, TCO=Total Cost of Operation, R=Revenue, NI=Net income

Net income accrued by Fazli variety of mango was Rs 2,96, 000 per hectare followed by Langra at Rs 2,81,500, Himsagar at 1,87,500 and Lasxmanbhog (1,20,000/ha).

8.6 Cash Flow Statement of Mango Orchards in Andhra Pradesh

Capital Cost/Invest Cost/Cost of Establishment of Andhra Pradesh

The cost of investment of mango orchard was estimated at reference year prices rather than at historical prices since majority (73 %) of the sample mango orchards were of more than 15 years of age and as such reliability of the historical cost would be questionable as it is fraught with memory recall bias and the farmers do not maintain any records of expenses made by them. The cost of investment of the mango orchards in the sample district, on an average, was estimated at Rs 31,750 per hectare during first year (Table 8.5). The cumulative cost of investment Rs 31,750 and maintenance Rs 30,750 till fifth year is reported at Rs 62,500 depending upon the quality of soil, irrigation and planting material.

Table 8.5: Average Cost of Establishment of Mango Orchard during First Year (per hectare) in Andhra Pradesh

Particulars	*Average Amount (Rs)*	*Share (%)*
Land Preparation	6,250	19.69
Manures and Fertilizers	6,000	14.90
Plant Protection	3,000	9.45
Planting Materials	3,125	9.84
Implement*	1,750	5.51
Fencing	3,125	9.84
Intercropping	4,750	14.96
Irrigation	2,250	7.09
Miscellaneous	1,500	4.72
Total	**31,750**	**100.00**

Source: Field data * Expenses on sprayers and other implements used

8.7 Cost of Maintenance (From 10 th year onwards) in Andhra Pradesh

Manuring, plant protection and irrigation are the major components in the maintenance cost, apart from the labor charges for various cultural operations such as weeding, input application, training, pruning etc.. The annual maintenance cost per hectare of full grown mango orchard (from 10th year onwards) has been worked out to Rs 13,750 (Table 8.6).

Table 8.6: Cost of Maintenance of Sample Mango Orchards in Andhra Pradesh (per hectare)

Particulars	*Average Amount(Rs)*	*Share (%)*
Labor	3500	25.45
Manures and Fertilizers	4250	30.91
Plant Protection	2000	14.55
Irrigation	2500	18.18
Miscellaneous	1500	10.91
Total	**13750**	**100.00**

Source: Field data.

8.8 Gross and Net Income of Andhra Pradesh

The average yield of mango varies from orchard to orchard depending on the climate, soil texture, cultivation practices adopted etc.. In case of the sample mango orchards in the study districts, the average yield was reported at 12.5 MT/ hectare in a stabilized orchard of 15 years and above. Considering the same yield, the economics of mango orchards has been arrived at for the average situation presented in table below:-

Table 8.7: Gross and Net Income from Sample Mango Orchards in Andhra Pradesh

Particulars	*Amount (Rs)*
Gross Returns @Average yield of 10 tones per hectare and selling price of Rs 4,500 per tone	56,250
Annual Cost of Maintenance	13,750
Net Income	42,500

Source: Field data.

Table 8.8: Cash Flow from Cultivation of Mango Orchard per hectare

Item	*Year*										
	1-5	*6*	*7*	*8*	*9*	*10*	*11*	*12*	*13*	*14*	*15-35*
Yield**	0	2.0	3.75	5.00	6.25	7.50	8.75	10.00	10.00	11.25	12.5
Gross income*	0	9000	16875	22500	28125	33750	39375	45000	45000	50625	56250
T. Cost	62500	10000	1000	11250	11250	13750	13750	13750	13750	13750	13750
N I	-62500	-1000	6875	11250	16875	20000	25625	31250	31250	36875	42500

Source: - Field data , Note *=Rs 4500 per ton, **= Metric ton per hectare, NI= Net income

8.9 Cash Flow Statement of Mango Orchards of Andhra Pradesh

The economics of mango Orchards in the sample districts was worked out the following assumptions as assessed during the study.

* Since the sample mango orchards were established without replacing any other crop, the pre development income of these lands was assumed to be zero.
* The mango orchard starts yielding from the sixth year on wards and stabilized yield is obtained from 15 year up to 35 year.
* The costs of maintenance of a mango orchard in the early years of planting is less than the matured garden, viz, Rs 10,000 per hectare (6th / 7 th year). Rs 11,250 per hectare (up to 9 th), Rs 13,750 per hectare (from 10th year). Variation is due to increase in nutritional and inter cultural requirements. The cash flow state in Mango orchard is brought out in the table 8.8.

The farmers in Chittor district were of the opinion that the recurring drought for the third consecutive year, viz, 2002-03, 22003-04 and 2005-06, had affected the economics of existing mango orchards.

8.10 Economics of Alphanso Mango in Sindhudurg, Maharastra

Capital Cost

The invest cost for raising Alphanso mango orchard is incurred during the initial five years of plantation. Such costs for cultivating the orchard in one hectare of land are given Table 8.9.

Table 8.9: Investment Cost per hectare of Alphanso Mango (in Rs)

Year 1	*Year 2*	*Year 3*	*Year 4*	*Year 5*	*Total*
79,408	34,674	34,676	19,228	14,936	1,84,996

Source: - Field data.

Maintenance Cost

Maintenance cost for initial five years has been capitalized. Thereafter the cost of maintenance keeps on increasing every year. However, for the purpose of arriving at the economics, the maintenance cost is grouped taking account the mean average maintenance cost. The details of maintenance expenses for raising one hectare of Alphanso mango orchard is given in Table 8.10.

Table 8.10: Cost of Maintenance per hectare of Alphanso Mango (in Rs)

	Year	
6 to 10	*11 to 14*	*15 onwards*
25, 104	25, 146	62, 760

Source: - Field data

8.11 Cash Flow Statement of Alphonso Mango

The cash flow statement for Alphanso mango orchard has been prepared on the basis of the following assumptions and information.

1. The capital cost has been taken as per accrual basis during the initial five years. It works out to be Rs 1, 84,996 per hectare with a mixed of those using blasting techniques and others.
2. The annual maintenance cost is Rs 573 for trees of 6 to 15 years old. The same for trees of more than 15 years old is Rs 641. Thus, the average annual maintenance cost comes to Rs 628 per tree.

3. Income has been taken as stable from 15 th year onwards. The income during 6 th, 7 th, 8 th 9 th, 10 th to 15 th year has been taken on the basis of actual yield and current price.
4. Net income has been arrived at after netting the maintenance and marketing cost from the gross income.
5. The economic life of the mango tree has been considered as 35 years, though it continues to give yields until it reaches an age of about 100 years.
6. The salvage value of orchards, being very low when considered for a period of 35 years, has been ignored.
7. Most of the Alphanso gardens in the state were raised in the 1980s under various schemes of state government and each item of expenditure was subsidized to a large extent. Therefore, subsidy component is ignored while computing internal rate of return (IRR) in the model projects.
8. The orchards are being developed in hitherto unused up lands/barren lands. The pre development income being negligible in the project area, the same has not been taken into consideration.

The Cash Flow Statement of Alphanso Mango Orchard (Rs per hectare) is given in **Annexure 25**. The facts that generation of income from the orchard starts from the sixth year of plantation and that income stabilizes from 15 year onwards are evident from the above Annexure.

8.12 Cash Flow Statement of Kesar Mango in Aurangabad

The cash flow statement of Kesar mango has been depicted in **Annexure 25.**

Capital Cost

The invest cost for raising Kesar mango orchard is incurred during the initial five years of plantation. Such costs for cultivating the orchard in one hectare of land are given Table 8.11.

Table 8.11 Investment Cost per hectare of Kesar Mango (in Rs)

Year 1	*Year 2*	*Year 3*	*Year 4*	*Year 5*	*Total*
44,649	18,118	21,005	24,615	27,857	1,36,244

Source:- Field data.

Maintenance Cost

Maintenance cost for initial five years has been capitalized. Thereafter the cost of maintenance keeps on increasing every year. However, for the purpose of arriving at the economics, the maintenance cost is grouped taking account the mean average maintenance cost. The details of maintenance expenses for raising one hectare of Kesar mango orchard is given in Table8.12.

Table 8.12: Cost of Maintenance per hectare of Kesar Mango

Year	*6 to 10*	*11 to 14*	*15 onwards*
Maintenance Cost (in Rs)	21,029	36,800	52,752

Source:- Field data.

8.13 Calculation of NPW, BCR and IRR in Selected Districts of Andhra Pradesh and Maharashtra

The mango orchard in the district was viable with the present level of yield, cost and price. The financial rate of return (IRR) worked out to 20.83 per cent (Table 8.13).

Table 8.13 : Calculation of NPW, BCR and IRR of Mango Orchard per hectare

S.N.	*Particulars*	*Value*		
		Chittor	*Sindhdurg*	*Aurangabad*
1.	Present Worth Discounted Cost (PWC) at 15 % of discount factor (Rs per hectare)	1,06,382	4,11,429	3,35,424
2.	Present Worth of Benefit (PWB) at 15 % of discount factor (Rs per hectare)	1,26,248	4,52,275	4,60,958
3.	Net Present Worth (NPW) Rs per hectare	19,866	45,846	1,25,534
4.	Benefit Cost Ratio (BCR)	1.19	1.11	1.37
5.	Internal Rate of Return (IRR (%))	20.83	17.66	23.21

Source:- Field data.

It is evident from the table that NPW registered highest figure at Rs 1, 25,534 per hectare compared to Sindhudurg (Rs 45,846 / ha) and Chittor (Rs 19,866/ ha). The internal rate of return was more than 15 per cent for all the sample orchards and as such the investment in mango is financially viable.

8.14 Sensitivity Analysis of Sample Orchards in Sindhudurg and Aurangabad of Maharashtra

Since there are wide fluctuations in production and prices of mango as per the grass root level situation in the study area, sensitivity analysis is attempted by increasing cost by 5 per cent and decreasing benefit by 5 per cent. The table below shows the details.

Table 8.14: Calculation of NPW, BCR and FRR of Mango Orchard per hectare

S.No.	Particulars	Value	
		Alphanso	Kesar
1.	Present Worth of discounted Cost (PWC) at 15 % of discount factor (Rs/ha)	4,32,000	3,52,196
2.	Present Worth of Discounted Benefit (PWB) at 15% of discount factor (Rs/ha)	4,34,411	4,37,910
3.	Net Present Worth (NPW) Rs per hectare	2,411	85,714
4.	Benefit Cost Ratio (BCR)	1.01	1.24
5.	Internal Rate of Return—IRR (%)	15.15	20.82

Source: Field data.

Under the sensitivity analysis, the BCR is more than one in both Alphanso and Kesar variety of mango. Thus, the investments in these varieties are beneficial. Similarly, the IRR s at 15.15 per cent and 20.82 per cent stand the test of sensitivity analysis. It is more than the threshold limit of 15 per cent reckoned for opportunity cost of capital.

9

Economics of Mango Processing

This chapter describes the processing aspects of mango, value chain involved in processing; economics of mango processing, problems associated with mango based prod UCTs etc In Section I attempts to work out economics based on field data collected during evaluation studies conducted in three states. Section two devotes to examine mango processing unit in the light of survey conducted by researcher in Chittor district of Andhra Pradesh. The paper in this direction was published in Indian Journal in Agricultural Economics recently. Further, reference was taken from the paper on "Economics of Mango Processing under Institutional finance —A case Study of Andhra Pradesh' published in Afro Asian journal by the author.

9.1 Section One

In Andhra Pradesh, 90 per cent of mango orchards are having Baneshan (Banganapalli) variety, which is not a pulp variety. Of the remaining 10 percent area, most of it is occupied by Totapuri (also called as Collector and Subarnarekha, which are suitable for pulp extraction. It is estimated that only 6 per cent of the total mango production is processed. Mangoes are processed into various types of products as maintained below.

Raw Mango Products: Pickle, Amchoor, Mango slice and Green Mango Beverage—-For pickles, the fruits are peeled, sliced into small pieces and mixed with 20 per cent salt, 7.5 per cent chilly powder, and 1 per cent asafetida on weight basis. Spices are then mixed in it and the slices dipped in boiled cool oil. The whole mixture is then kept for few days with frequent stirring and then filled in clean glass jars. Mango slices from peeled mangoes are dipped in solution of potassium meta-bisulphate (1.5 %) for 5 minutes and dried in sun or solar dehydrator. Amchoor is obtained by grinding the dried slices. Raw mango slices are dipped in 1.5 per cent potassium meta-bisulphate solution for 5 minutes, drained, mixed with equal amount of powder salt and stored in polythene pouches. These slices could be used later for the required food/ product preparation.

Whole raw mangoes are boiled with equal amount of water and pulp is extracted to one kg of extract, 1.6 kg sugar, 1.6 liter water, 80 gram salt, 20 gram mint, 10 gram cumin, 4 gram black paper and 20 gram citric acid are mixed. These mixtures is heated and filled in clean glass bottle. It may be used as raw mango squash, a modified version of 'Panna'.

Ripe Mango Products: Pulp, Mango Jelly, Beverages, Squash, Mango Leather—Fully ripe mangoes are washed, peeled and cut into slice. The slices are then homogenized into pulp, which is filtered through a sieve to remove the fiber. The pulp is heated to 76 -78 ^{0} center gate and to 2 gram citric acid and 2 gram potassium meta-bisulphate are added per kg of pulp. It is filled in sterilized glass/ jars and lids are sealed with wax. For mango jelly, mango is cut into 6 to 8 slices, the bulky juice is sent to sieve, seeds are separated and thick mango juice collected in wooden pot. Sugar or jiggery is mixed in 1.4 proportions. The preparation is subjected to natural drying process on bamboo-thatched beds. About 7 to 9 layers of juice is applied for natural drying every day and process goes for 25 days.

Mango juice may be prepared by mixing 1/ 3 rd of fresh or stored pulp with 2/5 th of water. Sugar and citric acid are added so that total soluble solid (TSS) and acidity of the product reach 15 and 03 per cent respectively. The mixture is heated to 95 ^{0} c filled hot in clean sterilized bottle. The bottles are sterilized for 10-15 minutes, cooled to room temperature and stored. Squash is prepared by mixing 1 kg of pulp with sugar syrup (1 kg sugar in 750 ml water). The whole mixture is heated to 76-78 ^{0}c and 25-30 gram citric acid added to it. The prepared squash is filled in sterilized bottle and stored. The homogenized mango pulp is taken and potassium meta-bio-sulphate is added to it @ 2 gram/kg of pulp. The pulp is then spread on trays smeared with butter and sundry. The process is repeated so as to obtain a thickness of 0.60 to 1.25 cm. Finally the dried product is cut into piece and wrapped in butter paper or polythene cellophane sheet. The different processing activities in the mango product chain are presented in following chart.

Waste Utilization—During the processing of mango, peel and stones are generated as waste, which is about 40 -50 per cent of fruit weight. They are rich in various nutrients and many value added products could be obtained from them. Good quality jelly grade pectin and edible fiber could be extracted from ripe mango peel Mango peel has lignocellulosic composition and hence its complete breakdown is difficult. Its composition depends on cow dung in 3: 1 ratio, which results in its successful biodegradation. Mango kernel contains high amount of fat and starch. The oil extracted from kernel is of good quality and could be used in cosmetic and

Chart 9.1: Different Processing Activities in Mango Product Chain

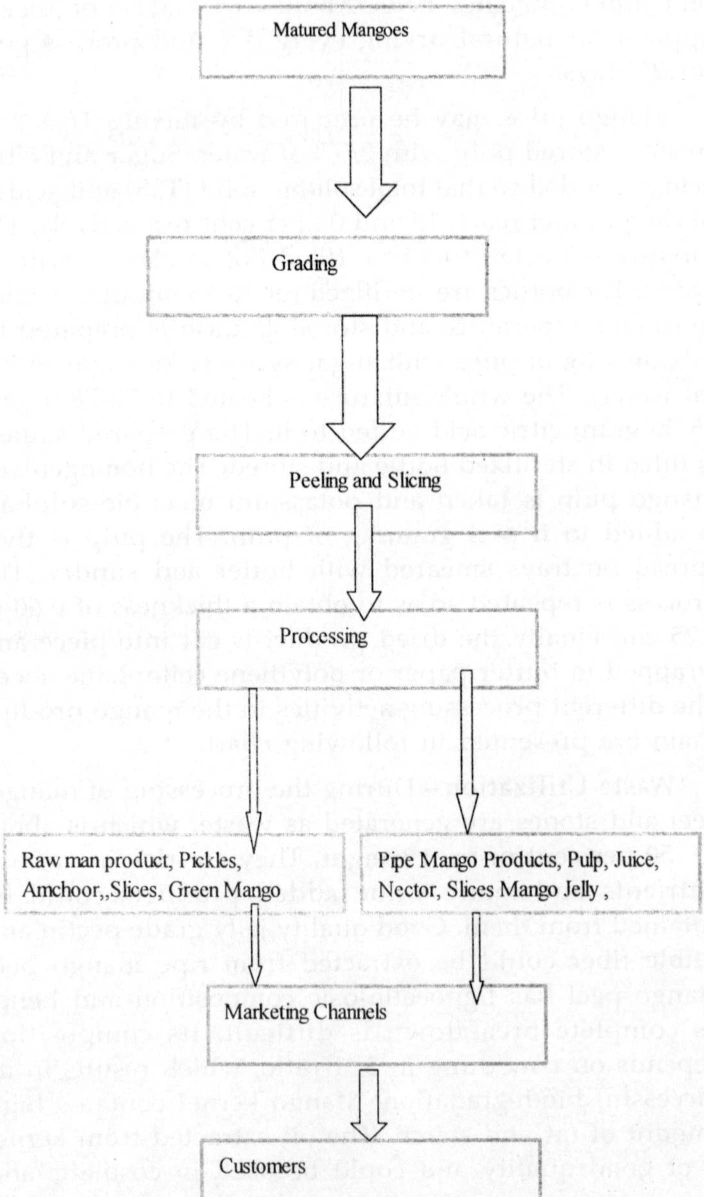

Chart 9.2: Flow Chart of Preparation of Mango Pulp

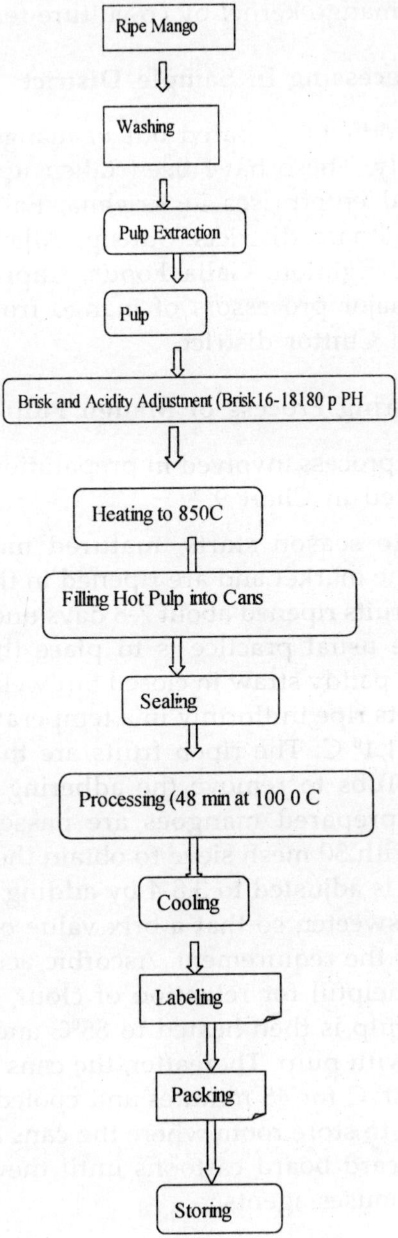

shop industries. About 10 per cent alcohol could be obtained from mango kernel by co-culture fermentation.

9.2. Mango Processing in Sample District

Major value products prepared out of mango are pulp, pickles and jelly. These have been taken up as village and house hold enterprises in Krishna, East Godavari and Vishakhapatnam districts. Sunsip, Allana, Vinsari, Fruitech, Jain Irrigation, Galla Foods, Capricorn Food Products are major processors of mango fruit pulp are concentrated in Chittor district.

9.3. Manufacturing Process of Mango Pulp

A flow chart of process involved in preparation of mango pulp is presented in Chart 9.2.

Once mango season starts, matured mangoes are brought from the market and are ripened in the ripening shed. Usually, fruits ripened about 7-8 days under tropical conditions. The usual practice is to place the fruits in single layers on paddy straw in closed but well ventilated rooms. The fruits ripe uniformly in a temperature ranges from 19.4^0 to 21.1^0 C. The ripen fruits are than washed with water in Tubs to remove the adhering impurities and dirt. The prepared mangoes are passed through pulpier fitted with 30 mesh sieve to obtain the pulp. The pH of the pulp is adjusted to 3.8-4 by adding citric acid. It may also be sweeten so that a brix value of 16-18 ^{0} is attained, as per the requirement. Ascorbic acid if added to the pulp is helpful for retention of clour, flavor and carotene. The pulp is then heated to 85^0C and sterilized cans are filled with pulp. Thereafter, the cans are sealed, processed at 100^0 C for 45 minutes and cooled. Then the cans are moved to store room where the cans are labeled and packed in card board cartoons until they are lifted by the export houses/agents.

9.4 Invest Cost of Pulp Making

The indicative cost for establishing mango pulping unit with an installed capacity of 600 tons of pulp per annum is about Rs 35 lakh, while for an aseptic unit the cost is estimated at Rs 2000 lakh (Table below):

Table 9.1: Indicative Investment Cost of Mango Pulp Units

Aseptic Packing Units			*Canning Units*		
Particulars	*Value (Rs in lakh)*	*Per cent*	*Particulars*	*Value (Rs in lakh)*	*Per cent*
Land Value –Lease	1.50	1.25	Land Value –Lease	0.10	3.04
Buildings	25.00	5.32	Buildings	15.00	28.69
Machinery	168.00	89.63	Machinery	15.53	55.70
a. Plastic Crates	0.30	0.16	a. Plastic Crates	0.13	0.46
b. Fruit Washer	2.50	1.33	b. Fruit Washer	2.00	7.17
c. Inspection Conveyor	1.80	0.95	c. Belt Conveyor	1.00	3.58
d. Screw Conveyor	2.00	1.06	d. Screw Conveyor	1.00	3.58
e.Pulper	2.50	1.33	e. Pulper	1.00	7.17
f. Rotor Pump	1.00	0.53	f. Rotor Pump	0.75	2.69
g.Boiler	3.50	1.86	g. Boiler	3.00	10.76
h. Genset	3.00	1.59	h. Kettles/Pasteurizer	2.45	8.61
i. Filtron Machine	2.00	1.6	i. Filling Tank &P. Lines	0.50	1.79
j. Star Aseptic	150.00	79.74	j. DS-24	0.50	1.79
ETP	8.00	4.25	k. Retards	0.10	0.36
Total	**203.0**	**100.0**	l. Generator Set	2.15	7.71
			ETP	3.50	12.55
			Total	**34.88**	**100.00**

Source: Field data.

9.5. Costs and Returns of Processing Mango into Canned Pulp

The length of operation of mango processing units depends

on the varieties of mango processed and source of procurement. For example, if the unit processes only the Totapuri mango produced in Chittor district, the fruits are available from the first week of June to the end of July (50-60days of operation). If the fruits of Totapuri are produced from Krishna District the length of processing could go up by another 15 days (from 15 May). Similarly, those units, depending on the orders received from the export houses, when processed Alphanso Mango, the fruits are available from April end onwards from Karnataka. Thus, the operation of these units is seasonal. With a view to increasing the operational days, the profit ratios, some of the units have been exploring the possibilities of processing other fruits and vegetables, such as papaya, tomato, guava, etc.

The average annual operational cost of a 600MT capacity pulp making unit was estimated to be about Rs 105.7 lakh (Table 9.2). The cost of production per tone and per kg of pulp worked out to Rs 12,858.50 and Rs 12.85. The canned units reported gross income of Rs 122.12 lakh and net income of Rs 16.42 lakh .The profit margin was arrived at 13.45 per cent in case of canned pulp making units.

Table 9.2: Costs and Returns of Processing Mango into Canned Pulp

Item	*Per (600 ton)/unit*	*Per ton*	*Per cent to total*	*Per Kg*
A. Input Cost (in Rs)				
i.Mango	6570000	9825	76.41	9.13
ii.Sugar	1008000	1000	7.78	0.88
iii. Citric Acid	165000	93.8	0.73	0.09
iv. Labor	1260000	633.92	4.93	0.63
2.Utilities (Electricity, Diesel etc.)	941864	784.89	6.10	0.62
3.Packing Material	*	*	*	*
Total Input Cost	9944854	11346.36	95.95	1139

B. Interest on Working capital (13% for 6 months)	625068	520.89	4.05	0.52
C. Total Cost (A+B)	10569932	12858.50	100.00	12.86
D. Gross Return (in Rs)	12211922	14856.01	-	14.86
E. Net Return	1641990	1997.51	-	2.00

Source: Field data, * Supplied by borrowers.

Packaging is an important component in canning. However, as all canned pulp units mostly do job work and after receiving orders from various houses, they need not incur any cost on packing. The export houses are supplying all materials for canning and packaging. Tin cans are made of thin steel plate of low carbon content lightly quoted with tin metal. The cans are lacquered inside with acid resistance gold colored enamel to seal microscopic spaces on the surface of ordinary tin can. Depending upon the requirement of the export houses, the cans are manufactured in situ in the processing units. Three sizes of cans namely 5.25 kg, 3.1 kg and 0.85 kg are extensively used by canning units for consignment.

9.6 Various Profitability Ratios

Various profitability ratios have been computed and presented in Table 9.3. These ratios measure the efficiency of canning units' activities, thus, identifying operating problems and strengths. The ratio of net profit to sales measures the earning capacity of caned firms. The ratio of expenses to sales indicates the extent of expenses that occurred in relation to sale and denotes the control of the management over the expenses. The ratio is indicative of the operational efficiency of canning firms. The high value of this ratio suggests that limited control is exercised over the expenses casting aspersions on the operational efficiency. The ratio of net profit to capital employed is a measure of return on investment and is a useful way of looking at the overall performance of the business. It indicates that performance can be improved either by generating more sales volume per rupee of capital employed or by increasing the profit margin of each rupee. However, the ratio (0.47) was not that encouraging for canning units. The capital intensity and limited scope of triggering demand for mango pulp posed as hurdle to improve the ratio. Further, the narrow margin (13.45%) in canned units (% of manufacturing cost to gross value to production) is an area of concern suggesting appropriate management of various cost centers for greater profitability.

Profitability Ratio of Canned Pulp Making Unit

Ratio of Expenses to Sales, Ratio of Net Profit to Sales, Ratio of Net profit to Capital Employed, Capital Output Ratio, Capital Employed Ratio and Manufacturing Cost as % to Gross Value of Production have been worked out in the table below:

Table 9.3: Profitability Ratio of Canned Pulp Making Unit

Particulars	*Value*
1.Total Cost (Rs in lakh)	105.70
2.Gross Return (Rs in lakh)	122.12
3.Net Profit (Rs in lakh)	164.42
4. Capital (Rs in lakh)	34.88
5. Ratio of Expenses to Sales	0.87
6.Ratio of Net Profit to Sales	0.13
7.Ratio of Net Profit to Capital Employed	0.47
8. Capital Output Ratio	0.29
9.Capital/Labor Employed	2.77
10. Manufacturing Cost as % to Gross Value of Production	86.55

Source: Field data.

9.7 Mango Jelly Cluster

Mango jelly is an age old industry in East Godavari district. It is mostly a seasonal industry functioning from May to July in a year.

Manufacturing of Mango Jelly— —Jelly is a semi solid product prepared by boiling a clear strained solution of pectin containing fruit extract free from pulp after the addition of sugar and acid. Pectin is the most important constituent of jelly. Usually, 0.5-1.0 per cent of pectin of good quality in the extract is sufficient to produce jelly. Pectin, sugar, acid, and water must be present approximately in the required proportion (i.e. pectin 1, sugar 65-70 5%, citric acid 1% and water 33.38%). The ripe mango fruits are cut into 6-8 slices by manual peeling. The bulky juice is sent to sieving. The sugar is sprinkled in to fruit extract while it is boiling to ensure complete dissolution. Well prepared mango pulp is spread on clean bamboo mats to form a sheet of 2 mm thickness. The size of the mat generally used is 1.35 m x 1.35 m. On its drying another layer is spread over this and allowed to dry, About 7-9 layers of pulp are applied for natural drying..The dried slab is cut into required sizes and packed for marketing.

9.8. Economics of Jelly Making

Generally, from one metric ton of ripe mango fruit, 350-400 kg of pulp used in jelly making is produced. The economics of sample jelly manufacturing units is presented below.

Table 9.4: Cost and Returns of Sample Jelly making Units

1.Particulars	*Per unit (Rs in lakh)*	*Per Kg (Rs.)*	*Per cent*
1.Input Cost(a-f)	2, 455	28.64	100.00
a. Mango	1, 500	17.50	63.31
b, Sugar	0.600	7.00	21.71
c. Labor	0.155	1.81	6.54
d. Consumables*	0.128	1.49	5.40
e. Depreciation	0.057	0.66	2.39
f. Interest	0.015	0.18	0.65
2. Gross Income	3.000	35.00	-
3.Net Income (2-1)	0.545	6.36	-

Source: Field data, * Mat, cloths, fire wood etc.

Average cost of production per unit and per kg of jelly was worked to Rs. 2.45 lakh and Rs. 28.54 lakh respectively. Net income has been arrived at Rs. 54,500 per unit and Rs. 6.36 per kg. Cost of production constitutes 81.83 per cent of gross income.

Various profitability ratios are computed and presented in the table below

Table 9.5: Profitability Ratio of Jelly Making Unit

Particulars	*Value*
1.Total Cost (Rs)	2,45,510
2.Gross Return (Rs)	3,00,000
3. Net Profit (Rs)	54,490
4. Capital (Rs)	85,000
5. Ratio of Expenses to Sales	0.82
6. Ratio of Net Profit to Sales	0.18
7. Ratio of Net Profit to Capital Employed	0.64
8. Capital Output Ratio	0.28
9. Manufacturing Cost as % to Gross Value of Production	81.84

Source: Field data.

The ratio of net profit to capital employed (0.64) was encouraging for jelly units that demonstrate efficiency in the use of capital with higher rate of return. However, profit margin (18.16%) in jelly making units needs to be further improved through appropriate management of various costs.

SECTION TWO

9.9 Overview of Mango Processing Units in Chittor District of Andhra Pradesh

The mango processing got momentum when an organized effort towards growth of the cluster was initiated during 1980 by M/s India Canning Center. This resulted establishment of 23 units between1981 and 1990. Subsequently, more units were established. As many as 56 units were installed between 1970 and 2006 (Naidu, 2002)

The wide range of investment has been made towards commissioning of mango units. The investment across different firms ranges from Rs 1 lakh to Rs1600 lakh (Table 9.6)

Table 9.6: Investment Pattern of Mango Processing Units in Chittor

Range of Investment (Rs in lakh)	*No of units*	*Per cent to total*
1.Up to 15	1	1.78
2.15-30	3	5.35
3.31-40	10	17.86
4.41-50	10	17.86
5.51-100	8	14.29
6.101-500	8	14.29
7.501-1,000	10	17.86
8.1,001-1600	6	10.71
Total	56	100.00

Source: Adapted Table 3 from KVReddy and Pramad Kumar's article, *Indian Journal of Agricultural Economics,* Vol. 65, No 2, April to June 2010, p. 282.

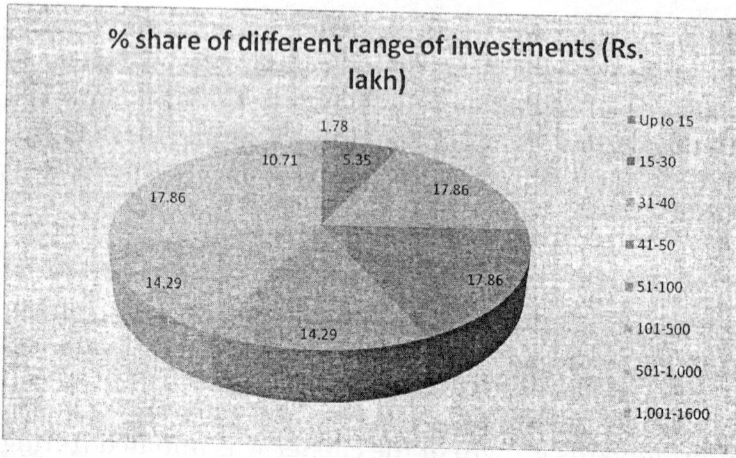

Graphic 9.1: Shares of Different Ranges of Investment Pattern of Mango Processing Units

About 11 per cent of the firms have an investment between Rs 10 to 16 crores falling in the category of large enterprises. While 18 per cent of the firm have an investment range of Rs 5 to 10 crore and fall in the size group of medium enterprises, the rest of the 72 per cent of the firms fall in the investment range of small and micro enterprises. The range of investment, however, is mainly associated with escalation of cost of investment rather than production capacity.

All the processing units in the district are covered under Fruits Products Order (FPO). The products such as pulp/ concentrate produced shall confirm to the FPO specifications as enunciated in Fruits Products Order, 1955; and Fruits Products Order, 1977.The large firms have also acquired HACCP certification. There are technological differences across the various size classes of firms.

9.10 Status of Export of Processed Mangoes in Chittor District

There is an increasing trend in export of both mango fruits and mango pulps in both quantity and value terms.

The export of mango pulp showed a quantum jump from 13 thousand tons in 1999-2000 to 120 thousand tons in 2006-07, revealing the importance of mango processing industry in the region. The low variability in the unit value realization in case of mango pulp as against the unit value realization of mango fruits seems to suggest the need for greater incentives for the processing sector. (Table 9.7),

Table 9.7: Export of Mango and Mango Pulp from Chittor District, Andhra Pradesh

(Quantity in tons, Value in Rs crore and Unit value in Rs per ton)

Year	*Fresh Mango Fruits*			*Mango Pulps*		
	Quantity	*Value*	*Unit Value*	*Quantity*	*Value*	*Unit Value*
1999-2000	275	0.55	20,000	13,538	25.72	18,999
2000-01	288	0.53	18,403	14,487	28.00	19,328
2001-02	540	0.99	18,333	16,785	37.00	22,044
2002-03	760	1.67	21,974	20,410	45.00	22,048
2003-04	360	0.67	18,611	22,413	49.31	21,999
2004-05	580	1.16	20,000	26,224	57.69	21,998
2005-06	600	0.60	10,000	95,360	190.72	20,000
2006-07	200	0.20	10,000	1,20,200	264.44	22,000

Source: Adapted Table 4 from K.V. Reddy and Pramad Kumar's article, *Indian Journal of Agricultural Economics*, Vol. 65, No. 2, April to June 2010, pp. 283.

9.11 Forward and Backward Linkages of Mango Processing Industry

The forward and backward linkages are very important from the point of view of farmers, processors and exporters. The mango processing industry is important for the economy of the Chittor district and that of the country as it has better backward and forward linkages. The prominent marketing channels for mango pulp in the study area are given below.

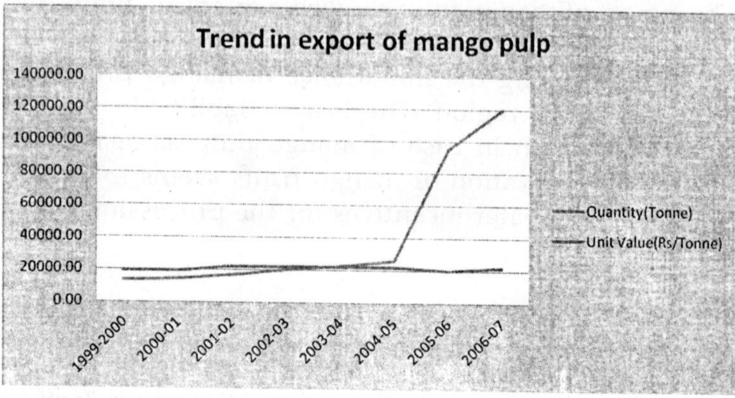

Graphic 9.2: Trends in Quantity and Value of Exports of Mango Pulp

Table 9.8: Forward and Backward Linkages of Mango Processing Industry

Backward Linkages	P	*Forward Linkages* ⟵
Producer—Pre-harvest ⟶	R	Firm using Pulp as input— —
Contractor— ⟶	O	Wholesaler of output Retailer -
Regulated Market — — — ⟶	C	Consumer Firm using Pulp as input-
Producer—Regulated Market ⟶	E	Exporting Output
Producer ⟶	S	Exporting Pulp
Distant Whole sale Market ⟶	S	Exporting Agencies—Exporting Pulp
Producer— —VillageTraders ⟶	O	Wholesaler—Retailer— —Consumer
Producer—Unregulated Market ⟶	R	

Source: Adapted Figure1 from KV Reddy and Pramad Kumar's article, *Indian Journal of Agricultural Economics,* Vol. 65, No. 2, April to June 2010, pp 284.

The processing industry is backwardly linked with six marketing channels basically to source the major raw materials i.e, mango pulp. Two of these channels are: (i) Producer— —Processor and (ii) Producer—Regulated market — —Processor, account for 80 per cent of total raw material by processing firms.

The mangoes required for processing are supplied directly by the orchards. Normally, these orchards were owned by the promoters of the processing units. The traders located in the Mandies are another important source of raw material supply. There are four major market yards set up in the district exclusively for mango trading in the session, located at Kattamanchi, Bamalcheru, Tirupathi and Puttur.

The processing industry is forwardly linked with five market channels. The two of these five channels, i.e., (1) Processor— —Exporting Pulp; and (2) Processor—Exporting Agencies—Exporting Pulp, account for about 85 per cent of the disposal of the mango pulp by the processors.

The small farms have lesser access to international market and depend heavily on the merchant exporters to export mango pulp on pre-contract basis. This has a bearing on the profitability of the processing units.

Table 9.9 Per Factory Capacity, Investment and Commodities Processed by Different Categories of mango Processing Farms

(Rs in crore)

Particulars	*Scale of Production*		
	Large Scale	*Medium Scale*	*Small Scale*
1. Capacity (tonnes)	13,000	52,200	2,000
2. Capacity Utilized (per cent)	75	50	50
3. Fixed Cost	15.00 (57.87)	6.00 (60.98)	2.0 (61.35)
4. variable Cost	10.92 (42.13)	3.84 (39.02)	1.26 (38.65)
5. Total Cost	25.92 (100.00)	9.84 (100.00)	3.26(100.00)

Commodities Processed Mango, Guava, Papaya, Vegetables
Mango and Guava Mango and Guava

Source: Adapted Table 6 from KV Reddy and Pramad Kumar's article, *Indian Journal of Agricultural Economics,* Vol. 65, No. 2, April to June 2010, p 285.

9.12 Economic Feasibility of Mango Processing Plants

Table below provides information on the capacity, investment, commodities processed by large scale, medium scale and small firms. The large scale firms processed different commodities namely mango, guava, papaya and vegetables. These firms work almost throughout the year, unlike medium and small scale firms, which are processing mango and guava fruits and work for three to four months in a year.

9.13 Employment Details

Employments details are depicted in Table 9.5.The large firms employ a large number of workers i.e, 700. The small firms on the other hands employ only 256 workers. However, most of the employment is on a part time basis, processing industry being a seasonal industry

Table 9.10: Employment Details of Different Categories of Mango Processing Firms

Employment	*Nature of Firms*		
	Large	*Medium*	*Small*
1.Executives	10	10	2
2. Managers	5	2	2
3. Workers			
(a) Full Time	100	-	6
(b) Part Time	600	500	250
4. No. of Months Operational	10	5	4

Source: Adapted Table 7 from KVReddy and Pramad Kumar's article, *Indian Journal of Agricultural Economics,* Vol. 65, No. 2, April to June 2010, p. 286.

9.14 Cost and Returns as well as Profitability Ratios

The cost and returns for the various size classes of processing firms are summarized in table below.

Table 9.11: Cost and Returns of the Processing Firms by Categories

Particulars	*Large*	*Medium*	*Big*
1. Mango Pulp(Tons) Avg/unit	5959	2280	860
2. Revenue from Mango Pulp	1214.40	446.25	131.25
3. Revenue from Guava Pulp	55.24	51.00	30.00
4. Revenue from Papaya	34.50	—	—
5. Revenue from Vegetables	57.50	—	—
6. Total Revenue (2+3+4+5)	1361.60	497.25	161.25
7. Fixed Cost	1111.42 (84.45)	413.77 (86.61)	123.12 (82.10)
8. Variable Cost	209.25 (15.85)	63.96 (13.39)	26.85 (17.90)
9. Total Cost (7+8)	1320.67 (100.00)	477.73	149.97
10. Net Return	40.93	19.52	11.25
Income Expenses Ratio			
a. operating Ratio	0.82	0.83	0.76
b. Fixed Ratio	0.15	0.13	0.17
c. Gross Ratio	0.97	0.96	0.93
Capital Ratio			
a. Capital Turnover Ratio	0.91	0.83	0.81
b. Rate of Return on Investment	0.027	0.033	0.056

Source: Adapted Table 11 page 288, *IJAE*, Vol. 65, No. 2.

It is observed that small firms produce 860 tons of mango pulp per unit whereas the large firms produce 5,995 tons. Total revenue generated, on an average, varies from Rs 161.25 lakh for small firms to Rs 1,361.6 lakh for large firms.Net revenue available for small firms was Rs 11.25 lakh and Rs 40.93 lakh for large firms. Thus, it is evident that the processing firms are profitable. The financial analysis ratio which includes income expenditure ratio and capital ratio were computed to further understand operational efficiency of these firms. The operating ratio ranges from 0.76 for small firms and 0.82 for large firms. This signifies that in every rupee of gross income, a substantial portion of operation cost is incurred. The fixed ratio varies from 0.13 for medium firms to 0.17 for small firms. Relatively large share of gross income is used for meeting the fixed expenses. The gross ratio is less than one signifying the efficient operation of firms. However, it is substantially high and varies from 0.93 for small firms to 0.97,for large firms. This reveals that a large portion of gross income is utilized for meeting the total expenses. It also reveals that small firms are more efficient than other size class of firms.

The capital turnover ratio ranges from 0.81 for small firms to 0.91 for large firms revealing that every rupee investment by small firms generates gross income of 81 paisa. This measures show that large firms are more efficient than the small firms. The rate of return on investment gives a better picture of efficiency. The value of rate of return on investment varies from 0.027 for large firms to 0.056 for small firms showing that every rupee of capital investment generates a net return of 3 paisa and 6 paisa. This measure shows that small firms are more efficient than large firms.

9.15 Feasibility of Mango Processing Units

All the three class of firms are feasible as per NPW and BC Ratio criteria. The BCR of small firms is higher than that of large firms for all discount rates. This reveals that small firms rank higher than large firms. Table shows the details.

Table 9.12: Feasibility of Mango Processing Units

D.F(% age)	*Large*		*Medium*		*Small*	
	NPW	*BCR*	*NPW*	*BCR*	*NPW*	*BCR*
10	679.5	1.07	159.1	1.04	129.6	1.11
12	399.5	1.04	66.8	1.02	86.4	1.08
15	72.4	1.01	-40.6	0.98	35.9	1.04
20	-219.5	0.96	-135.3	0.94	-9.6	0.98

Source: Adapted Table 12A, page 289, *IJAE*, Vol. 65, No. 2.

The feasibility mango processing units using the criteria of internal rate of return (IRR) and pay back period.

It is observed that IRR of small firms (19.31%) is the highest followed by that of large firms (17.5%) and medium firms (13.87%). All three size class of firms is available as their IRR is greater than the opportunity cost of capital. Thus, the small firms rank the highest and the medium firms rank the lowest as per the FRR criteria. Table depicts the details.

Table 9.8: Feasibility of Mango Processing Plants

Feasibility Measure	*Large Firms*	*Medium*	*Small*
IRR (%)	17.50	13.87	19.31
Payback Period (Years)	5.99	6.89	5.25

Source: Adapted Table 12B, page 290, *IJAE,* Vol. 65, No. 2.

9.16 IRR, Pay Back Period etc.

The payback period explains the number of years in which the investment is paid back by the project. It is observed that investment in mango processing plant has least payback period for small firms (5.25Years) followed by that of large firms (5.99 years) and medium firms (6.89 years). The shorter payback period for mango processing plants provides an important opportunity for an entrepreneur.

The break even analysis helps the entrepreneur in taking managerial decision as to what should be the level of operation of the firm. Both the variable cost of production and the output price per ton of processed products is the lowest in case of small firms and highest for the large firms (9.10). The large firms have access to the international markets; whereas the small firms depend on merchant exporters to dispose the product in the international market. The large firms adhere better to the quality standards demanded in the international market as compared to small firms. These are the major reasons for the differential in the output prices across the firm size groups.

9.17 Break Even Analysis

Table 9.13: Break even Analysis for Mango Processing

(in Rupees)

Particulars	*Scale of Operation*		
	Large Scale	*Medium Scale*	*Small Scale*
1. Price per ton of Processed products	22712.26	21889.21	18750
2. Variable Cost of Processed Products/ton	18539.16	18147.71	14316.63
3. Money Terms (Break Even Point—BEP)	113885016	38096825.9	11353519
4. Quantity Terms—tons -BEP	5014.25	1746.82	05.52

Source: Adapted Table 13, page 290, *IJAE*, Vol. 65, No. 2.

The breakeven point for small firms (Rs 113.54 lakh) is the lowest followed by medium firms(Rs 380.97 lakh and the large firms (Rs 1138.85 lakh) respectively. The BEP in physical terms for small firms with 605.52 tons is the least followed by medium and large firms with production of 1746.82 tons and 5014.25 tons respectively. It is implied that firm should operate at a level generating gross revenue and producing output above these values by the respective firm size classes to be profitable.

10

Post-harvest Management, Exports of Mango Based Products and Performance of Excise Zone

The present chapter analyzes the post harvest management of mangoes for exports, and export performance of mango and mango based products. The role of AEZ has been also explored.

10.1. Post Harvest Management of Mangoes for Exports

Mangoes are generally harvested at physiological mature stage and ripened for optimum quality. Fruits are handpicked and plucked with a harvester. The best way to observe maturity in mango is color of the pulp, which turns cream to light yellow on maturity. The harvesting needs to be done in the morning hours and fruits should be collected in plastic trays and kept in shades. The fruits harvested with 8-10 mm long stalks appear better on ripening as undesired sports on skin caused by sap burn are prevented. Such fruits are less prone to stem-end rot and other storage diseases. A simple, low cost and portable mango harvesting device has been propagated by AEZ, Krishna costing Rs 2,000, which is subsidized by 50 per cent. The post harvest losses in mangoes have been estimated in the range of 20-30 percent from harvesting to consumption stage (Table 10.1).

Table 10.1: Post harvest Losses at Various Stages and Different Crops in Andhra Pradesh

Stage	*% of Losses*	*Crop*	*% of Losses*
1. Field Level	10	Grape	25
2. Transport	5	Mango	20
3. Packing	2	Pomegranate	10
4. Storage	9	Sweet Orange	20
5. Processing	4	Banana	30
6. Total	30	Sapota	22
		Onion	25

Source: S. Mahendra Dev and N. Chandrasekhara Rao (2004), "Food Processing in Andhra Pradesh—Opportunities and Challenges", Working Paper No-75, June.

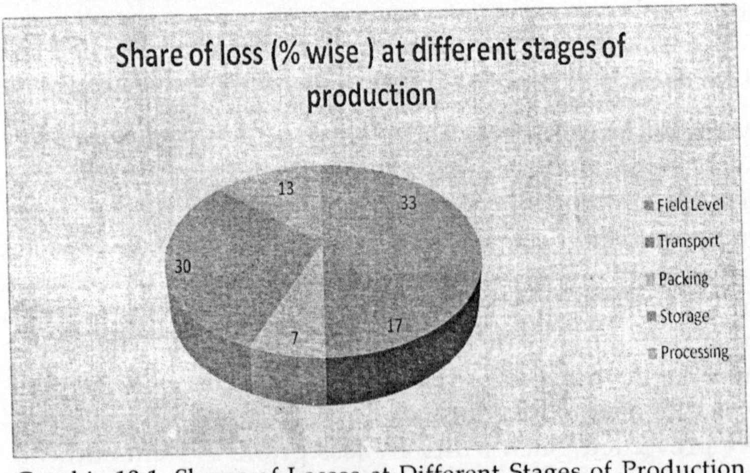

Graphic 10.1: Shares of Losses at Different Stages of Production

Grading—In order to reduce value loss and to remove the field heat, the produce should be harvested during coolest part of the day, i.e. in the morning. A preliminary grading is done immediately after harvesting at the field level. The mangoes are graded according to size and maturity.

Desapping—Matured mangoes exude large amount of sap from the cut stem. As the sap contain lots of resorcinol(oil), which burns the mango skin if contracted by the sap, the mangoes are desapped by placing them in framework in an inverted position for two hours to completely remove the sap from the fruit.

Processing—After the desapping process, the mango is processed in a post harvest treatment line having following operations in a common facility center (pack house).

10.2 Post Harvest Operation

Pack house/Grading and Packing Center

A pack house is a place where products are brought after harvesting to prepare them as per the market requirements, in terms of washing, brushing, waxing, grading, packing, cooling etc. It also carries out value addition without modifying the appearance of the product. The shelf life of the product is enhanced by providing the congenial conditions. Keeping in view the variety of crops, two to three grading and sorting lines may be installed. After sorting, the produce is packed in various desired packs and pre-cooled. The operational steps in the pack house would be as under:—

Sorting, Cleaning and Washing—A preliminary storing of produce is carried out to remove un marketable prices and foreign matter such as plant debris, soil, stone etc.. before the produce is passed on for further operations. Cleaning and washing are carried out with flush of cold water to clear produce which has acquired latex stains from injures caused during harvesting.

Fungicide Treatment—As decay caused by molds/ bacteria is a major cause of loss of fresh produce during the distance transportation and marketing, the fungicides are applied after the produce is washed and dried. The fruits are taken to a trough containing detergent and 0.5 per cent fungicidal solution. After treating the fruit with the detergent and diluted fungicidal solution (Binomial powder), the fruit is wiped off with muslin cloth till dirt and latex stains are completely removed. After treatment with the fungicidal solutions, the fruit is dried with dry muslin cloth and spread on the grading table and air-dried.

Size, Grading and Waxing—The fruits so treated are finally graded according to the size, maturity and quality without any blemish. Selection and grading in a small packing house are best done by human eye and by hand and assisted by sizing rings. For long distance destination the fruit is treated with wax .The wax emulsion is kept in a vessel and a muslin cloth is soaked in it and applied on individual fruit. This is carried out to enhance appearance and limit water loss from produce.

Packaging—The fruit is packed in corrugated fiber boxes (CFBS) with necessary bursting and puncture resistance and compression strength. The specification details of CFB boxes are recommended by APEDA

Pre-cooling —After packaging the mango in CFB boxes, the packed cartoons are placed in the pre-cooling rooms where the temperature is set at 12.5^0 C with 90-95 percent relative humidity. Once produce is placed in pre-cool, it will radiate heat to the room by virtue of field heat and heat of respiration. As soon as the produce is brought to its optimum storage temperature, the respiration will be brought under control and the maximum storage life of the produce be realized. It is observed that the fruit pulp temperature comes down from 35^{0}Cto 12.5^{0}C in about six hours.

10.3 Cold Storage

After pre-cooling, the produce is brought to cold storage to extend its shelf life. The harvest fruits are pre cooled to 10-12 0 C and then stored in an appropriate temperature. The fruits of Dashehari, Mallika and Amrapalli are pre-cooled at 12^0 C and then stored 8^0C with 85-90 per cent relative humidity. The fruits can be stored for 3-4 weeks in good conditions and at low temperature. The development of cold storages, including cold chain, for transport has an important role to play in reducing post-harvest losses. The bio chemical and microbial changes are slow at low temperatures. As such, refrigerated cold storages used to prolong the shelf life of perishable produce. The fruits can be stored for 3-4 weeks in good condition at low temperature. The problem of chilling injury at low temperature can be overcome by keeping the fruits in 0.5 per cent ventilated polythene bags.

Transportation—The truck has been adopted as the most convenient mode of transport due to its easy approach from the orchard to the market. However, these trucks are not found suitable for transporting these live materials as they exert lot of pressure on the fruits and do not boss temperature control devices. Therefore, it is imperative to design and develop suitable transport system. Refer containers (Refrigerated vans) may be found useful for long distance transport and export purposes, as they would help in reducing the post harvest losses. The processes in post-harvest management of mangoes are depicted in Chart ahead.

Chart 10.1: Flow Chart of Post –harvest Operations of Mango Export

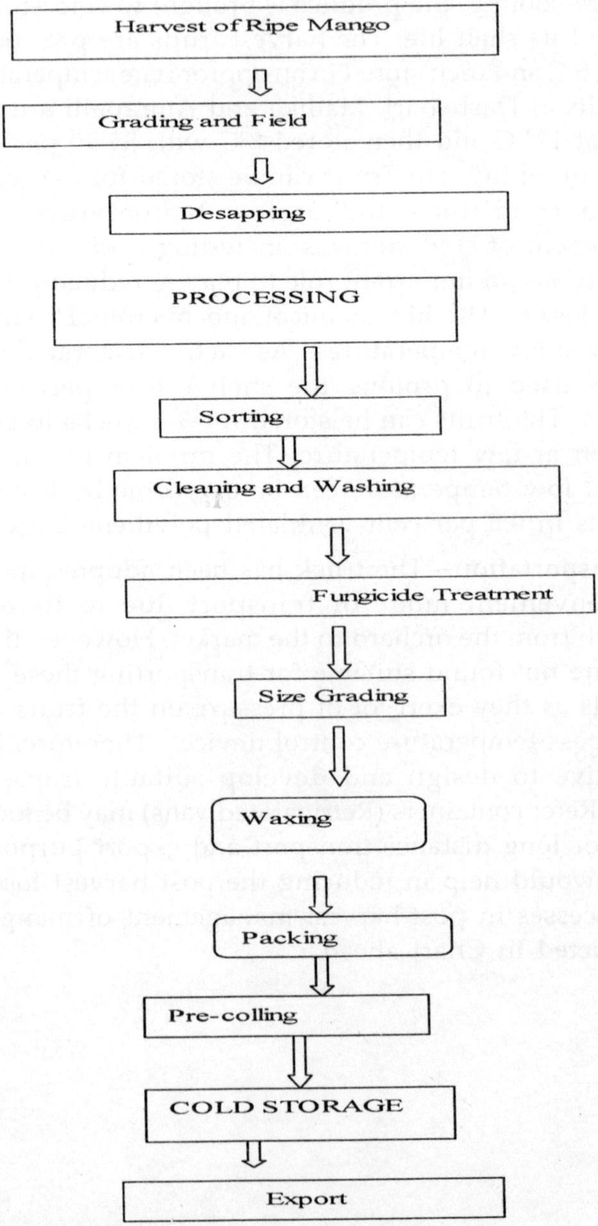

10.4 Export Performance of Mango

Fresh Mango— —As stated earlier that the quantum of fresh mango exported from India in 1987-89 was 20.30 thousand metric ton which enhanced to 83.70 thousand metric ton in 2008-09. In terms of value realization it was Rs 23.24 crore in 1987-89 and Rs Rs 120.5 crore in 2008-09. Share of export to production was about 1.5 per cent.

Mango Pulp—As regards mango pulp, on an average, India export about 105 thousand metric ton worth Rs 390 crore.

Other Mango based Products—India's export of mango and mango-based products during 2004-05 registered a marginal growth of 6.62 per cent over the previous year (Table 10.2).

Table 10.2: India's Export of Mango/ Mango based Products to Major Markets during 2002-03 to 2004-05

(Rs in Crore)

Country	*2002-03*	*2003-04*	*2004-05*	*% change*
Saudi Arabia	103.96	86.82	103.12	18.77
UAE	66.88	69.09	54.72	-20.80
Netherland	42.41	40.50	49.16	21.38
Bangladesh	13.89	35.36	29.20	-17.42
UK	36.68	25.25	25.62	1.47
Kuwait	20.24	19.22	16.04	-16.55
Yemen Republic	28.32	18.23	34.07	86.89
USA	19.44	17.14	15.38	-10.27
Japan	9.45	7.33	14.42	96.73
Nepal	8.07	6.15	5.66	-7.97
Lebanon	7.62	5.42	6.37	17.53
Oman	5.67	5.48	6.07	10.77
France	9.73	3.69	7.71	108.94
Total	**468.87**	**436.01**	**464.89**	**6.62**

Source: APEDA.

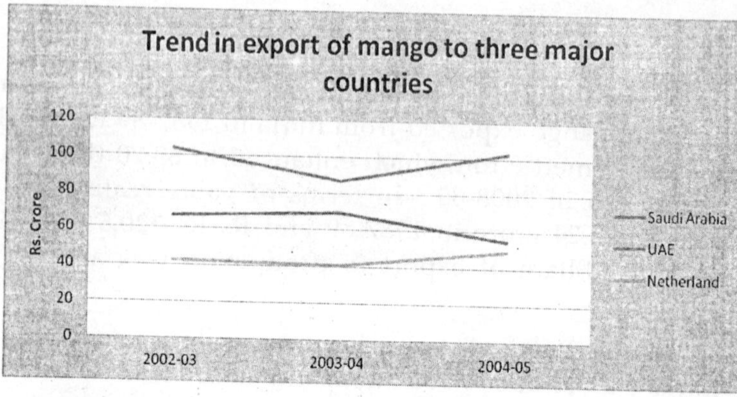

Graphic 10.2: Exports of Mango in Three Major States

Saudi Arabia continues to be largest market for Indian Mango and mango based products. Export of this market in 2004-05 registered a steep growth of 18.77 per cent over the previous year when the same reached a level of Rs 103.12 crore as against Rs 86.82 crore. The other markets showing a sharp growth during the period comprised: France (108.94 %), Yemen Rep (86.89 %), Netherland (21.38%), and Lebanon (17.53%). On the other, the countries representing decreasing trend during the period included: UAE (20.80%), Bangladesh (17.42 %), and Kuwait (16.55 %).

10.5 Export Prices of Mango and Mango Pulp

APEDA, since its inception in 1986 has been playing a major role in the export effort of Mango and Mango based products. They provide various services to the trade and industry. These include identification of new markets, regular participation both national and international trade fairs and also vigorously launching of promotional campaigns for mango and mango based products like mango pulp, juices, chutney and pickles. The computation of the ratio of FOB price at Chennai as collected from exporters in both the study districts to the international border prices shows that both mango pulp and fresh mango are highly price competitive in the international market. Table below shows the details.

Table 10.3: Export Competitiveness of Mango/ Mango Pulp

Items	*Prices during 2005-06*			*Ratio of Domestic*
	FOBP (USdollar)	*Chenni (Rs.)**	*DP(Rs) #*	*Price (DP) to FOB Price(FOBP)*
Fresh Mango—Alphanso	1820	80080	18000	0.225
Neelam	1000	44000	8000	0.182
Banganapalli	1600	70400	4500	0.064
Mango Pulp – Totapuri	900	184186	23000	0.125
Alphonso	1050	214884	—	—
Raspuri	900	184186	23000	0.125

Source: Exporters from Chittor and Vijaywada, * US dollar is converted to rupee @ Rs 44 per US dollar, , # Standard price at which the processors procure mango from various Market Yard in Chittor and Vijaywada.

11

Supply Chain Management and Credit Support

Supply chain management (SCM) represents the management of entire set of production, manufacturing/ transportation, distribution and marketing activities by which a consumer is supplied with a desired product. The practice of SCM encompasses the disciplines of economics, marketing logistic and organizational behavior to study how supply chains are organized and how institutional arrangements influence industry efficiency, competition and profitability. One can also include the production practices in the field to understand food safety and traceability (Ramaswamy).

11.1 Supply Chain Management (SCM) in Mangoes

Supply Chain System (SCS) for mangoes covers a balanced and efficient relationship encompassing input supply, production, harvesting, storage, processing, marketing export etc. of mangoes. It also manages such relationship in a collaborative and efficient manner to garner optimum benefit. Out of it for all the players are in the chain.

Agri-Export Zone—Considering the existing production of mango and mango pulp as well as future potential for facilitating supply chain management, the AEZs for mango and mango pulp were notified in 2002.However, there is no significant development in linkages, both back ward and forward and no breakthrough in developing quantity standard and post harvest management for furthering exports. Number of mango pulp making units, production of mango pulp as also export of fresh mango and pulp have picked up in Chittor AEZ. However, the infrastructure in terms of post harvest facilities like pack-houses, cold storages, etc have not come up to exploit the potential. In mango AEZ in Krishna district, as against the target of 25 pack-houses only two have come up. Only one post harvest facility is available at AMC,Vijaywada (Gollapudi). Export of fresh mango from Krishna district has always been below 500MT per annum. Currently, export of mango by air is in passenger air craft, due to which the freight charges are very high. There are mango growers' cooperative organizations and they have not been able to plan an organized production and marketing system. They have also not been able to reduce the marketing channels. These channels are so long increasing the margins to the middle men and thus aggravating marketing efficiency. In order to facilitate the SCM, the Govt. of Andhra Pradesh had sanctioned a scheme for promotion of export of mangoes through mango growers Cooperative Organizations'. As a pat of the scheme, a cold storage plant was set up in 1993 as 'Post-Harvest Temperature Management Scheme' at AMC, Vijaywada. Exports were taken up under the management of Marketing Department during the initial years through reefer container by sea and air. However, the progress in export front was not that encouraging (Table. 11.1).

Table 11.1: Performance of Post harvest Management Unit at AMC Vijaywada

Period	*Avg quantity Exportd (MT)*	*Average Service Charges Collected*	*Avg. Expenses Incurred*	*Countries Exported*
1993-2001	143.82	1.70	7.33	Singapore,
2002-2006	124.20	0.61	5.81	Dubai,
				Hong-Kong, Malaysia

Source: Field data.

The AMC Vijaywada was charging nominal service charges from exporters. The unit has the facilities of one cold storage plant with 20 MT capacities, two pre-cooling units each with a capacity of 20MT.

Vijaya Association of Fruits and Vegetable Growers, consisting of 230 members in Vijaywada, have been engaged in export of mangoes since 1994. They have been using the pack house and cold storage unit at Golapudi AMC. They use the protocol developed and given by Central Food Technological Research Institute (CFTRI) for export through central marketing fund of mango. Further, as the protocol for sea shipment has not yet stabilized, APEDA engaged a scientist from Belgium to develop a protocol for cases where more than 15 days sea journey is required. Vitas Company Export Private Limited, Chennai visits AMC Gollapudi every year and also visit the mango orchards and purchases the fruits at the ripening stage. The graded mangoes are priced at Rs 15,000 per MT and are of good size and quality ("labeled as garden Fresh Mangoes")

Marketing—In both the districts, exclusive mango market yards are functioning for marketing of produce. There is also excellent net work of traders both local and up country, commission agents etc. to assist the smooth flow of the product (fruit) from growers to final consumers. However, even though growers/traders Associations are informally functioning in both the districts, these have not taken up any initiatives to reduce the large margins eaten by the middle level functionaries. They have not made any attempt even to reduce the length of the marketing channels. Such growers associations have not made any visible attempt in creating awareness with regard to quality in improvement in fruits. However, conduct of "Mango Festival" has been a regular affair in Chittor that creates a lot of awareness among the growers/ traders /processors on quality issues.

Growers'/ Processors' Federation——In order to smoothen out the SCM for mango processing sector, 'Chittor District Canners' Federation was formed during 1991. Later it was rechristened as Chittor District Fruit Processors Federation. The Federation used to assist units in hazard analysis and critical control point (HACCP) Certification with assistance from APEDA, modernization of cluster to Andhra Pradesh Industrial and Technical Consultancy Organization (APITCO), seek soft loan and subsidy with APEDA, Ministry of Food Processing Industry (MFPI), National Horticulture Board (NKB). The details of National Horticulture Mission are given in the **Appendix –2.** In consultation with Pollution Control Board (PCB) and other technical institutes, the Federation helps the units in formulating exact technology to treat liquid and solid affluent wastes.

The Federation of Farmers' Association (FFA), an authorized body to address the issues of mango growers in consultation with the government of Andhra, managed to form six exclusive mutually aided cooperative societies (MACS) of mango growers of Chittor District. The Agri-Terra of Netherlands, through the FAO, the FFA and Horticulture Department of Andhra Pradesh has initiated the project and helping the farmers to develop these cooperatives. The cooperatives are expected to result in an additional value of up to 20 percent to the growers as they cut second-rung traders/commission agents from the supply chain y providing a direct inter face between the buyer and seller. Besides making it easier for companies to enter into agreements, these MACS are expected to strengthen the hands of mango growers. The tie-up would result in saving of transportation charges and market cess. The idea is to strengthen the supply chain and facilitate a direct linkage between the corporate buyers and farmers (Kurmanath, 2007). On its part the FFA would give training to the farmers' issues such as pesticides and improving quality.

Input Supply—As far as input availability is concerned, for growers —plant materials are available sufficiently in Srikalahasthi, Tirupati, Mallavalli in the study district. All sorts of pesticides and chemicals are locally available in major towns. Processors procure mangoes directly from mandi, growers, factory, and tradrs. Generally processors go for a storage capacity of 7 days fruit requirement to match with the ripen cycle.

Power supply by Andhra Pradesh Transmission Corporation (APTC) is quite adequate to run th units. Diesel generating unit have been installed to meet power requirements during shut down. Water, being a major requirement for processing unit, is available sufficiently at site. A good network of transport arrangements is provided to transport both raw materials and finished products. Both sea and air transport is available at Chennai, which is only 185 km from Chittor and 300km from Vijayawada.

Various enzymes like bio-tropilase enzyme for consistency of mangoes are being purchased from M/s Biocon, Bangalore. Citric acid (for maintaining the pH level of the pulp), ascorbic acid (added as per customers' requirement) are being arranged from Bangalore and Chennai. Various machineries required for installing the canning unit are Plastic Crates, Fruit washer, Belt conveyor, Screw conveyor, Pulper, Roto pumps, Boiler Kettles/ Pasteurizer, Flanger, (to seal one side of the tin),Embosser (for labeling).These are available in Chittor and Bangalore.

Another important input in the pulp industry is the packaging and packing material, such as cans, aseptic bag, and cartons. The units undertaking the processing on job work basis are supplied with require can material, labels, and packing materials by Export Houses which have provided production orders. Aseptic packing sizes are mostly of 200 litre [228 kg double strength(DS) or 215 kg single strength (SS),] 45 kg, 54kg, and 91 kg depending buyers specification. Mostly DS aseptic packages go to Europe and USA. The SS aseptic packages are supplied to Coca-Cola, Indian Fruit Juice Manufacturers like Pepsi, Parle, and Godrej. Cans are mainly supplied to Middle East Countries like Saudi Arab, (Dubai, Yamen, Kuwait), Korea, Japan, Singapore, Australia etc.

Table 11.2: Crop Loan for Maintenance of Mango Orchards by Sample Bank Branches

(Account in number and Rs in lakh)

Year	*Crop Loan*		*Of which Mango*		*Percentage*	
	Account	*Amount*	*Account*	*Amount*	*Account*	*Amount*
2003-04	10452	883.83	3786	396.76	36.22	44.89
2004-05	12214	1190.19	4818	560.92	39.45	47.13
2005-05	16303	1756.18	6306	836.85	38.68	47.65
Overall	**38969**	**3830.20**	**15070**	**1814.03**	**38.67**	**47.07**

Source: Indian Bank, RRB and DCCB.

11.2 Credit Support –Andhra Pradesh

Data collected from a sample of 10 bank branches (3

branches of Indian Bank, 5branches of Regional Rural Bank and 2 District Central Cooperative Bank) revealed that crop credit to mango during the last three years constituted a share of 38.7 per cent of total crop loan accounts and 47.1 per cent of total crop loan amount in Table 11.2.

Pre-harvest contractor, VT/CAs are adequately provided with' Secured Over draft' facility from banks. They utilize the same in lending to farmers as also in going for lease / contract of mango orchards. Bank loan is also utilized by them for procuring mangoes from the field as also from the market in order to supply to up country traders, as there remains time lag of 30-75 days while getting payments from UPCTs. Similarly, term loan for establishment of mango orchards constituted 19.1 per cent of the total Agricultural Term Loan (ATL) Account and 17.2 per cent of the ATL amount during the period 2003-06 (Table 11.3). However, interactions with banks revealed that bankers are not inclined to provide term loan owing to its long term tenure, up to 10 years.

Table 11.3: Agricultural Term Loan for Establishment of Mango Orchards by Sample Bank Branches

(Account in number and Rs in lakh)

Year	*Agr. Term Loan*		*Of which Mango*		*Percentage*	
	Account	*Amount*	*Account*	*Amount*	*Account*	*Amount*
2003-04	42	19.87	21	13.25	50.00	66.68
2004-05	227	124.3	33	20.25	14.54	16.29
2005-05	281	240.16	51	32.6	18.15	13.57
Over all	550	384.33	105	66.1	19.09	17.20

Source: Indian Bank, RRB and DCCB.

The company after procuring the fruits from the growers/professionals suppliers route the entire sale proceeds through their bank accounts. The system is so long as there is smooth flow of the margin to the growers after adjusting their repayment. However, the growers complained that the company delays the payment resulting in late repayment of loan by growers. All processing has working capital arrangements with banks, which range from Rs 20 to 60 lakh depending on their requirements. Banks work out the working requirement based on Nayek Committee recommendations.

11.3 Credit Support –Maharashtra

The short term loans for maintenance of Alphonso mango orchards have been availed from bank in the district and same shows increasing trend. In all the sample cases, farmers availed bank credit for maintenance of the orchards especially after introduction of KCC scheme. A part of requirement has also been met by purchasing inputs on credit from suppliers and availing advance from traders cum middlemen (Dalals). Progressing farmers are invariably availing bank loans, but small farmers normally lease out their orchards to farmers cum traders and receive money in advance to meet the maintenance expenses till fruiting stage. Out of the 25 sample beneficiaries, bank loan particulars in respect of 12 farmers have been collected, which are given in Table 11.4. Most of the sample farmers used a part of the KCC limit for Investment in Mango Orchard.

Table 11.4: Availment of Bank Credit by Some Sample Beneficiaries in Sindhhudurg, Maharashtra

Sample case No.	*No. of Trees*	*Financing Bank/Branch*	*Purpose/ Activity*	*Loan (Rs.)*	*Bank loan/ hectare*
1	800	SDCCB, Vengurle	KCC	2,00,000	25,000
2	200	SDCCB, Vengurle	KCC	55,000	27,500
3	1000	SDCCB, Vengurle	KCC	7,40,000	74,000
4	300	SDCCB, Vengurle	KCC	1,85,700	61,900
5	125	SDCCB, Vengurle	KCC	1,27,000	1,01,600
6	1050	BOM, Jamsandha	WC	2,00,000	19,048
7	1600	BOM, Jamsandha	KCC	6,50,000	40,625
8	150	RSGB, Mutal	KCC	50,000	33,333

9	800	RSGB, Mutal	KCC	5,00,000	62,500
10	850	RSGB, Mutal	KCC	40,000	4,706
11	1780	BOL, Vijaydurg	TL	6,00,000	33,708
12	1500	RSGB, Mutal	KCC	3,00,000	20,000
Total	10155	—	— —	36,47,700	25,920

Source—Bank, Note—Kisan Credit Card, WC=Working capital, TL= Term Loan.

It is observed from the above table that average annual maintenance cost of mango orchard up to plucking stage comes to Rs 62,700 lakh as per the current package of practices. However, loan actually availed by the farmers was at Rs 35,920 per hectare. It also revealed that in the reference year, the bankers assessed the loan requirement at Rs 600 per tree for meeting maintenance expenses and accordingly sanctioned KCC limit of Rs 60,000 per hectare. It was gathered that the remaining portion of the maintenance cost was met out of own funds and/or by availing credit from the traders-cum- middlemen and input dealers on terms, which restricted free marketing. This indicates there is ample scope for bank finance.

11.4. Repayment Performance of Bank Loan

The repayment performances of all the sample farmers were good as all the loans were standard. Moreover, bank loan was not available for trees taken on lease. The bank loans were disbursed in the district during last three years for mango cultivation is given in table ahead.

The apathy of farmers towards bank loan is primarily due to the fact that alternate options for arranging maintenance expenses are in practice in the district. At times, the input agents provide inputs on credit and collect their dues in harvesting season. But traders cum middle men, who normally lift the produce through their local agents, are continued to be the primary source of finance of the farmers. These traders cum middle men provide advance ranging up to 20-30 per cent of the anticipated production at the door steps of the farmers, during October to January, without going through elaborate documentation. Farmers reported no interest was charged till settlement of yearly account in June. However, interest is charged @ 2 per cent per month on the outstanding balance, if any, of the advance after pattis are settled around June.

Table 11.5: Details of Bank Loan Disbursed to Mango Growers in Sindhudurg, Maharashtra

Particulars	*2003-04*	*2004-05*	*2005-06*
Productive Area Under Mango (hectare)	15,847	19,000	20,100
Assessed Credit Requirement (Rs in lakh)	45625	780.00	2654.60
Of which,			
Long Term	146.25	180.00	210.61
Short Term	310.00	600.00	2444.00
Bank Loan Disbursed (Rs in lakh)	1476.98	2216.03	2195.30
Of which,			
Long Term	131.37	422.91	520.56
Short Term	1345.61	1793.12	1674.74

Source: Potential Linked Credit Plan of Sindhudurg, 2007-08, NABARD, Maharashtra Regional Office.

11.5 Credit Availability

Unlike Sindhudurg district, raising mango orchards in a commercial manner is a recent phenomenon and mostly orchards are being raised with own resources or availing personal loans. Specific credit limits for cultivating mango orchards alone have not been availed from any bank by the sample cases. However, bankers in the district are inclined to sanction credit limits for growing Kesar mango orchards and meeting maintenance expenses. As already indicated, since Kesar mango orchards are coming up in the district on a large scale, there is potential for dispensation of bank credit in future.

12

Constraints, Issues, Strategies and Policy Suggestions

This chapter outlines identification of constraints, chalking out issues, evolving strategies and formulation of policies.

1. Constraints

i. Cultivation Aspects

Field study revealed that availability of genuine plant material is lacking. Thus, small and marginal farmers are often deceived. Despite large wealth of mango cultivars available, none of the cultivars have all the qualities like precocity, dwarfness, prolificity, regularity in bearing, resistance to pest and diseases etc. However, adequate efforts have not gone in to developing improved varieties of mango trough breeding. Further, efforts were hardly attempted to popularize the hybrid varieties and educate the growers and consumers on such varieties.

The study also observes that orchard management is not proper among many of the farmers. Improper spacing not based on soil type, variety, rainfall/ irrigation etc. giving rise to poor yield is common. Endevours are yet to make to rejuvenate the old orchards through new plantations. Certain farmers followed a blanket fertilizer doses which are not based on soil type, irrigation and plant conditions. Several mango orchards have been intercropped with paddy, which has resulted in good yield in the beginning. This may create several problems at a later stage like low yield, decline fruit quality and increased mortality of mango trees. Inundation and chloride injury had started leading to leaf burning, twig drying and outbreak of diseases.

Mango does not bear a good crop every year and tends to follow alternate bearing pattern. However, there is no effort to minimize irregular bearing by adopting suitable cultural practices, like open canopy management, pruning, adequate manuring etc.

Fruit drop has been a problem for certain farmers. They opined that even after careful farming mangoes were infected with spots (mangu diseases), which did not fetch remunerative prices. However, in most cases, the farmers tended to take the advice of the local fertilizer/ pesticide dealers for its control, which often failed. Application of recommended doses of plant growth regulators at the appropriate stages of fruit growth, following of proper plant nutrition, plant protection measures and cultural practices, especially irrigation schedule, could greatly reduce the fruit drop.

ii. Inadequate Extension Services

Field study observes that there is lack of training and awareness creation on various cultivation practices for producing good quality mango. Growers cultivate mangoes just for the sake of cultivation and they have no adequate knowledge on good agricultural practices. Horticultural officers are not adequately posted in the district for providing the required extension services. The Horticulture Department always has been facing shortage of staff. There is inadequate awareness on post harvest needs and its technology among the mango growers and traders.

iii. Infrastructural Bottlenecks

It has been reported that more than 20-30 per cent of the produce is lost in the post-harvest operations. This is mainly because of factors like non-availability of proper infrastructure in terms of facilities for handling the produce, poor transport and storage facilities. For distant markets and exports, infrastructure in the form of pack houses with automatic sorting, washing, waxing, packing, pre cooling, storage and marketing has not developed commensurate with the level of production and export prospects. To address few of the issues and for giving further boost to the exports of fresh mangoes from the state, especially in the light of opening of mango exports to Japan, action has been initiated by the Department for establishment of 2 vapour heat treatment plant center, one each at Nuzvid (Krishna district) and Tirupati. Andhra Pradesh Agros has been identified as the Nodal Agency for establishing these units. The government is also contemplating to develop a Horticulture Hub, with an end to end approach, under private-public partnership at Nuzvid in Krishna district, at an estimated cost of Rs 28 crore. Thus modalities are being worked out.

The poor transportation and road condition coupled with inappropriate packing and temperatures as high as 40^0 C further deteriorates the qualities. The prices of mangoes in international market fluctuate on daily basis and long period of journey reduces the freshness as also realization for mangoes.

The present position of post-harvest handling is not up to the mark. Even grading standards are not uniform and limited to a few varieties and that are not mandatory. Only Agricultural Marketing Committee (AMC), Gollapudi is having one unit with facilities of cold storage, processing hall for hot water drip treatment etc.

iv. Lack of Export Promotion and International Competition Strategies

Generally, International trade demands mango varieties that are with fiber-less flesh, good aroma, attractive color, (preferably red ,pink, purple or yellow) and better sugar and acid blend. Efforts are not being made to produce and grade our mango based on such tastes and varieties. Therefore, export strategy should be to respond to the choices of the consumers of the importing countries. Fresh mangoes are now one of the most liked tropical fruits in the United States. Per capita consumption doubled from 1.1 lbs per person in 1995 to an estimated 2.2 lbs in 2004. The US imported 638 million lbs of mangoes in 2004 at a cost of 196 million dollar. Mexico (63%), Peru (11%), and Brazil (9 %) were the major supply countries to the USA market.

The mango marketing seasons in various countries is given in **Appendix** 3. India's major marketing season is April to July, where as it is produced round the year in Brazil, Colombia, Kenya and Venejuela. The season is quite long in Burkino Faso, Costa Rica, Indonesia, Jamaika, Mexico, Nicargua and Peurto Rico. Very big mango orchards of a single variety of the size ranging from 2,000 to 10, 000 ha area have come up in those countries, keeping an eye on export market which require consistent bulk supply of uniform good quality.

Many African and Latin American countries have become major suppliers to European market. Philippines (70 %) is the largest supplier to Japan, having invested heavily in vapour heat treatment technology to ensure that export variety of the "Manila Super" could be certified as fruit fly–free by Japanese quarantine inspectors. Australia exports its "Kensington Pride" variety to Japan after winning Japanese health authority of its vapour heat treatment programme. Pakistan gives higher subsidies, charges low freight tariff and also its proximity to Gulf countries has given it's 'Ratual' mango a permanent place in eating table in the gulf. Therefore, our efforts for mango exports need to be re-christened with well plan strategies.

2. Issues and Strategies

A number of issues need to be addressed to strengthen mango crop so as to cater to the export demand of mango and mango based products in India.

a. Growers

i. Fruit size and Shape Improvement

Under-nourished trees cannot exhibit correct shape and size of the fruits. For optimal development of the fruit, location specific nutrient management schedule with optimal doses need to be developed and provided to the farmers. Hit and miss method as followed by certain farmers may not serve the purpose. Canopy management need to be stressed to be achieved the desirable leaf size. In the study area it was observed that average age of the orchards is more than 40 years and the inter plant spacing ranged from 12-16 m.

ii. Uniformity of Shape and Color Exhibition

An attractive shape is always appealing to the buyer. Color development and bright exhibition are possible through exposure of the fruit to solar light and temperature, which means canopy management, adequate nourishment and stage of harvest. Early harvests always lack good color development on ripening.

iii. Blemishes/Scars on Fruits

Different types of blemishes and scars on the fruit make it unattractive for marketing and get rejected while grading. Various causes for the occurrence of blemishes/ scars need to be identified and suitable remedial measures may be taken up to reduce such occurrences. The Indian Agricultural Research Institute (IARI), New Delhi has introduced to mango varieties which have an acidic-sweet taste and also develop a technology to prevent infection of mango fruit by insects. These two mango varieties Pusa Arunima and Pusa Surya , with characteristics such as appropriate acidic-sweet blend, golden color of the pulp and a cylindrical nut, would help the country in competing with Philippines in mango exports to Europe.

b. Exporters and Traders

i. Export Promotion Strategies

Concerted efforts need to be stepped up to intensify export promotion efforts. Some of the points, which merits attention of the policy makers in this respect include (i) strengthening infrastructure base, (ii) efficient post harvest management, (iii) better improved packaging,(iv) excluding new markets, (v) improving cold storage and transportation logistics (vi) developing India brand mangoes and campaigning abroad about the quality, (vii) promoting an efficient export marketing net work to optimize our export and (vii) setting up of more quality control laboratories in the export processing Zones. Exploring new export destinations has to be the priority. Japan has opened up its market by lifting its 20- year-old ban on Indian mangoes in June 2006. Banganapali, including other exportable varieties can now be imported by Japan. Chinese market also needs to be tapped by our mango farmers.

ii. Post harvest Infrastructure

The success of post harvest consideration depends upon the identification of appropriate technologies, sourcing and creation of need- based infrastructure, followed by its proper management. With the post harvest losses roughly pegged at 25-30 per cent of the production level (8.86 lakh MT) in the study area, it implies wastage of 2.7 lakh MT. The volume of production (even at the farm gate price of Rs 4, 500 per ton) results in a loss of Rs 122 crore of revenue to the mango sector.

Since the creation of post harvest infrastructure requires huge capital investment initially, its creation has to be considered on merit so that proposed infrastructure remains in operation for at least 200-250 days in a year. Creation of collection centers with facilities of sorting, grading, transport and marketing in nearby urban areas requires to stressed. Such facilities could be created by a group of farmers growing mango by forming a cooperative society or a association of farmers or self help group (SHGs). Some AMCs are contemplating to strengthen the existing market and post harvest handling infrastructure by utilizing the subsidy assistance from the Ministry of Agriculture, government of India through the scheme for development / strengthening of Agricultural Marketing Infrastructures, Grading and Standardization.

Pack Houses—For distant market and exports, establishment of pack houses with automatic sorting, washing, waxing, packing, pre cooling, storage and marketing on large scale could be considered by public and public sector. These facilities could be made available on hire basis of the farmers. Certain criteria like, urban areas with concentrated pockets of production , having good connectivity, availability of electricity and water round the year, hygienic surroundings etc, need to be considered for setting up of pack houses. The pack houses need to have the adequate capacity and should have the position pre cooling unit/cold storage. Provision of refrigerated/insulated van to have cool chain up to marketing may also be considered in the pack house with the aim to market quality graded products.

Cold Storage—The development of adequate cold storage capacity with latest technology/ cool chain would help not only in increasing the self life and minimizing post harvest losses through proper storage but also help farmers in taking timely marketing decision. Cold storages with multi-chamber/ multi-commodity concept need to be popularized. Environment friendly and modern cooling system need to be introduced at par with some developing countries.

Vapour Heat Treatment Plan—There is the need to establish one vapour heat treatment plant (VHPT) to sort out the problem of fruit fly, which is the main hindrance for exporting mangoes to Japan, USA and European countries. There should be the provision for the export of mangoes in modified atmospheric containers.

Rail and Road Transport—-Mangoes are transported trough trucks, open pickup or bigger trucks. Specialized transport vehicles should be used, which may have separate cabins and partial shade so that losses during transport minimized. Around 300 trucks take mango to upcountry market every day during the season (April-May) from Nunna market yard in Vijayawada. Mango is also sent through a special wagon from Nuzvid rail way station. For export purpose, mango is being transported to Chennai air port. Gannavaram air port near Vijayawada required to upgraded and cargo flights need to be introduced for mango.

Capacity Building— There is shortage of trained and skill man power for the management and operations at field level. There is need to create world class firm/ mango orchards for which capacity building needs to be initiated. An effective technology transfer system (ETTS) may be promoted to take up technology development/ transfer to the mango growers/ processors.

c. Processors

Mango pulp making units put forth a lot of their grievances during the field study. As almost all canning units are operating on work order basis, export houses give only 50 per cent of the cost of advance. Rest is paid after the consignment is lifted in phases, which may go up to 6-7 months. Processors' money remains locked and they pay interest to banks on their borrowings. Further, because of competition and inconsistent international prices, exporters are offering un attractive conversion charges(Rs 22000\MT of pulp). Thus, most of the units are operating on reduced net margins (Rs 200/MT of pulp).

Processors requested for a rationalization of sales tax rates. As per the existing structure, sales tax rate @I2.5 per cent is lived if the pulp is manufactured and sold within the state of Andhra Pradesh. However, the same is only 4 per cent if the pulp is sold in other states or that manufactured in other states in is sold in Andhra Pradesh. With regard to paying of 1 per cent market cess to the AMCs on the procurement of mangoes, this is waived by the government if the end product is exported or deemed as exported. However, this benefit has not been received by many of the processing units. Similarly, the subsidy on power tariff as announced under the Food Processing policy of the state government has not reached many of the units, as reported. Because of stiff competition from the large corporate units, increasing cost of manufacture, which are not adequately compensated by the job charges being paid by the export houses, many of pulp units in the small scale sector are under the threat of becoming sick. It was also observed that for exporters, the interest charged by the banks under EPC is 7-8 per cent, where as small scale processing units are charge at 12-13 per cent interest per annum. Exporters viewed that shipments by sea are not preferred due to unreliable sea protocols. Freight charges for Singapur, Dubai and Middle East is at Rs 50 / kg now. However, there is no air freight subsidy for mangoes. A few other facilities required in Chittor district as revealed by processors are setting up of a common solid waste treatment facility, warehousing facility, to avoid carrying the produce to Chennai etc. The Marketing department may also conduct extensive studies and provide information to the industry on a continuous basis on the demand and international market prices.

d. Marketing

The study revealed that middle men are considered as necessary evils in the marketing system. Two types of measures need to be directed for controlling the activities of middlemen. These are (i) regulating the marketing of mango, (ii) creating alternative channels of trade for marketing for mango.

It is known fact that the present commission levied by the commission agents is nearly 4-10 per cent of the total value. But the commission charges fixed under the APMC Act of state may be 1 to 1.5 per cent. To correct the situation it is necessary to have a dialogue with the traders and fix a reasonable commission (4-6%), which may partly be born by sellers and buyers instead of sellers alone paying it as at present. This type realistic approach may give results in getting the markets regulated and prevent other losses in weighing, handling etc.

It is suggested that creating producers co operative organizations will solve most of the problems and increase the bargaining power. But marketing is a specialized activity and producer cooperatives consisting of small growers can not undertake the job. So it is necessary to create marketing organizations, which can take care of marketing as well as trade in mango. The main features of the organizations may include establishment of collection centers at growing regions and regulation of all buying/selling activities through the organizations at the market yards. Further, registration of all buyers with the organizations, advancement of loans on the pledge of produce, disbursement of inputs through collection centers and arrangements with banks for providing production loans are other features of the organization. For maintaining the organization, a commission of 4-6 may be charged. The department of horticulture (DOH) can be closely associated with the organization and some responsibility of collection centers can be entrusted to their field staff as happened in case of MAHAMANGO, a federation of mango producers, societies in Maharashtra, promoted by Maharashtra State Marketing Board. The horticulture departments of the respective states like Andhra Pradesh and West Bengal may conduct detailed survey on its functioning and assess the scope for formation of such intervention.

e. Institutional Credit

The credit requirement of mango is very high. Presently middle men meet the part of the requirement of the credit for which the farmers market the produce through the middlemen. Therefore, to shorten the activities of the middlemen in the marketing channel, it is necessary to provide the credit required by the growers. At present, though the banks are advancing the credit, it is limited to production of crop / establishment of mango orchards. However, the Sindhdurgu credit does not cover the marketing cost. This can be achieved if the marketing organizations through its assembling centers arrange to supply the inputs on credit basis on the understanding that the producer through its assembling centers sell through that marketing organizations. These organizations may suggest the banks located in area to route the credit through them. As the assembling centers of the organizations will be distributing the credit in kind and cash components, there will be less scope for misutilization. The repayment will also be regular as the producing industry is marketed through organization.

4. Policy Suggestions/Action Points

1. Growth and sustainability of small farms is important as they constitute about 75 per cent of total mango orchards selected. Since the small mango growers are viable, the support and incentive should be given so that they over come the competition due to opening up the economy
2. The mango processing industry should be supported as the unit value realization of mango pulp is more stable than that of raw mango. It also has a number of forward and backward linkages benefiting the economy of the region.
3. Contract farming should be promoted to ensure timely and adequate supply of raw materials and to minimize the cost of raw materials. It will minimize the marketing margin in the supply of raw materials of the processing industry.
4. Domestic consumption ought to be promoted through campaigns and by producing diversified products to serve as a cushion to the mango processing industry against fluctuations in the demand at the international markets.
5. The cooperative societies should be set up to help the small firms to increase their access to the international markets and realize higher price for their output.
6. Small firms are poor in adopting the adequate quality standards and the technology used are not favoring the market. This calls for the support and nurturing by government to help technology up-gradation and to adopt Hazard Analysis Critical Control Point (HACCP).
7. Government should promote the production of mango and other horticultural commodities in the

region to promote the adequate supply of raw materials through out year for increasing the capacity utilization of firms.

8. The mango being a potential horticulture crop needs to be developed by adopting a cluster approach. The Department of Horticulture may categorize the districts in to specific clusters and 9. There are several varieties which need to be identified and given a geographical identity. Such varieties are dependent upon specific soil and climatic conditions. The department of horticulture may identify and make efforts to clean out the places linked with particular variety of mango and there after attempt for registration of geographical identity of such local varieties. Branding in such a way that it would lead to integrated growth of that crop'.

10. Considering the existence of senile and unproductive orchards mainly in Krishna district (20 %) Andhra Pradesh; Murshidabad (30 %), West Bengal and Sindhudurg (30%), large scale replantation needs to be initiated to rejuvenate such orchards. Improved root stocks need to be introduced and strategies required to be finalized to promote high density planting of mangoes. The department of horticulture may popularize the improved package of practices among the growers and ensure the new plantations are established.

11. The study revealed that availability of genuine planting material of the required quantity is lacking. It is learnt that bankers are reluctant to offer term loan on account of non availability of adequate planting material. The DoH may take necessary action and ensure that adequate and good quality mango is available for new mango plantation. Sometimes there has been a demand

in certain quarters to create Horticultural Crops Planting material Authority (HCPMA) for ensuring quality of planting material.

12. It is believed that alternate bearing has been creating problems in mango production to a large extent. While in one year it creates glut in with excess production, the next year it results in short supply due to low production. This resulted high price of mango, which affects processing units with high cost of production. The crop production can be regulated to a certain extent through pruning immediately after the harvest followed adequate manuring, judicious irrigation and effective plant protection measures. The appropriate package of practice may be popularized by the DoH of the selected districts of the states.
13. There is increasing need to set up pack houses with washing, waxing, packing, pre cooling and storage including refrigerated vans for transport at the production centers. The pack houses need to be designed in such a manner to facilitate year round operation, taking into consideration the availability of other perishable products in the region. These should be linked with terminal markets.
14. There is the need to establish one vapour heat treatment plant (VHPT) to sort out the problem of fruit fly, which is the main hindrance for exporting mangoes to Japan, USA and European countries. There should be provision for the export of mangoes in modified atmospheric containers in ships.
15. Mango processing industry, particularly pulp making, has enough potential to grow in the future. This is because of the fact consumer preferences

to-words synthetic drinks have been declining due to growing health consciousness and increase in purchasing power. Jelly and pickles making has also immense potential to grow. Proportionately, production and productivity of good quality/ processing worthy mango has to increase for which availability of adequate institutional credit is essential. Credit is required for crop establishment and maintenance, installation of on- farm infrastructure, such as drip irrigation, processing units, export credit etc. Banks to provide adequate credit to various segments of mango industry, keeping in view the banking plan / potential envisaged in Potential linked credit plans (PLCPs) by NABARD.

16. The credit purveyed to the mango sector is not getting reflected in the present system of data generation by banks. There is a need to streamline data on credit flow to mango separately for various activities, especially in the AEZs. Credit flow in AEZs may be included as an item of agenda in the district level and state level banker's meets.
17. Further, the data on area, production and yield also need to be streamlined after conducting proper survey. Data generated by the department and other agencies at the field level vary to a large extent. Similarly, there is a need to streamline the data and put in place a system to update and publish the data on market arrival and prices of mango variety-wise.
18. There is need to regularly review and monitor the progress and various issues confronted by the stake holders in AEZs at the state/ district levels to identify constraints and initiate corrective actions.

19. Marketing cycle of Alphanso mango in Maharashtra mango is being done almost entirely on credit. The traders, commission agents, exporters, retailers, etc operate in the cycle only on credit and the farmer receives his proceeds only after it is realized from the ultimate consumer. In the process the middle men get the lion's share of benefit from the investment of the primary producer. Therefore, adequate bank credit must reach the farmer in the entire cycle.

20. Less than 5 per cent of total mango produced in Sindhudurg and Aurangabad districts in Maharashtra is reported to be processed. Further, lower quality mangoes sold for processing fetch less price. There is an immediate need to scale up the volume of processing, to increase shelf life of mango and better the return by suitable value addition. A few farmers are processing at a limited scale with this end, which is required to be upscale with suitable domestic policies.

21. Exporters purchase quality mangoes from markets as also directly from the farmers. Except for a few big farmers, other farmers are not aware that their produce is being exported. Registration of export orchards, on the lines of grapes in Maharashtra has not picked up. It needs to be expedited by the Agriculture Department.

23. The self help groups (SHGs)/Farmers Clubs of mango farmers in selected districts of Maharashtra could organize mango festivals with the help of their counter parts in other districts. The mango farmers can be taken on study tours to other places for awareness and skill.

References

1. http;/www.horticultureworld.net
2. National Horticulture Mission
3. National Institute of Nutrition (NIN), Hyderabad.
3. *Indian Journal of Agricultural Economics,* Vol. 65,No. 2, April-June Issue, An Economic Appraisal of Mango Processing Plants of Chittoor district of Andhra Pradesh by K.V. Reddy and Promod Kumar pp. 277-297.
4. Atteri, B.R. (1994), "A Study of Physical and Economic losses of Dasheri Chausa Varieties of Mango in Delhi Market", *Bihar journal of Agricultural Marketing,* Vol. 2, No. 4, pp. 325-329.
5. Josi, M.G., S.S.Wadkar, P.D.Veerkar and A.G. Power (1999),"Comparative Economics of Scale of Processing Alphonso mango in to Pulp in South Konkan Region", *Bihar Journal of Agricultural Marketing,* Vol. 7, No. 2, pp. 190-194.
6. Naidu, P.D. (2002), Survey Report on Mango Production and Marketing in Chittoore district, ATMA,NATP, Chittoor District, Andhra Pradesh.

7. Suryaprakasa Rao (1993), "Mango Processing Industry in Andhra Pradesh", Paper presented at workshop on Mango Production, Processing, Marketing, and export by Peddy Reddy Timma Reddy Foundation, November 1993, Hyderabad.

8. Consultation Workshop on Export Prospects of Indian Mangoes, Organized by NABARD on 23, February, 2005, Mumbai, Paper on Present Status of Export of Mango from India by Dr R.D.Muley, Director Horticulture, Maharashtra State

24. G.D. Banerjee, "Marketing of Mango processing under Institutional Finance—A case Study in Andhra Pradesh," *Afro Asian Journal of Rural Development,* July-December 2001,Vol. 34, No. 2.

25. G.D. Banerjee, All Hands on Deck, September-October Issue, 2002, *Times Agriculture Journal, The Economic Times* and NABARD,

26. G.D. Banerjee, Horticulture— An Over View Poised for Golden Revolution – November-December Issue, 2002, *Times Agriculture Journal, The Economic Times* and NABARD.

27. G.D. Banerjee, Impact of Agro Processing Industry on income and employment of Small and Marginal Farmers, *Indian Journal of Agricultural Economics,* Annual Conference, 2002.

28. Ramaswamy, C. (2007), Supply Chain Management in Agriculture: Trends Status, Initiatives by Tamil Nadu Agricultural University, paper presented in the 8 th Agricultural Science Congress held at Tamil Nadu Agricultural University, Coimbatore, India,15-17, February, 2007.

29. Kurmanath, K.V. (2007), "Mango Growers join hands to gain more values", http://www.thehindubusiness line.com/2007/02/23 stories/

Annexures

Table 1: Nutritive Value per 100 Gram Mango

Nutrients	*Ripe Mango*	*Green/Raw Mango*
Protein (g)	0.6	0.7
Fat (g)	0.4	0.1
Minerals (g)	0.4	0.2
Fiber (g)	0.7	1.2
Carbohydrates (g)	16.9	10.1
Energy (kcal)	74	44
Vitamin C (mg)	16	3
Total carotene (mcg)	2,210	90
Beta carotene (mcg)	1,990	NA
Potassium (mg)	205	83
Sodium (mg)	26	43
Calcium (mg)	14	10
Iron (mg)	1.3	0.33
Phosphorus (mg)	16	19

Source: National Institute of Nutrition (NIN), Hyderabad.

Table 2: State-wise Number of AEZ, and Number of District Covered with Name

State	Number of AEZ	Name of the districts covered
Andhra Pradesh	5	Krishna, Chittore, Rangareddy, Medak, Mehboobnagar, Vijayawada, Hyderabad etc. (10)
Maharashtra	2	Ratnagiri, Sindhudurg, Thane, Ahmednagar, Raigad, Aurangabad, Beed, Jalna, Latur (9)
Uttar Pradesh	1	Saharanpur, Muzaffarnagar, Bijnaur, Meerut, Baghpat, Bulandshahar, Jyotiphulenagar, (7)
Gujarat	1	Ahmedabad, Khed, Anand, Vadodara, Surat, Navsari, Bharuch, Narmada, (8)
West Bengal	1	Malda, Murshidabad (2)
Tamil Nadu	1	Madurai, Dindigul, Virdudhunagar, Tirunelveli, Teni (5)
Bihar	NA	NA
Total	11	42

Source National Horticulture Mission.

Table 3 : Area, Production, and Yield of Mango to Total Fruit Crops during1987-88 to 2008-09

Year	Area (in thousand hectare)	Percentage to total area under fruit crops	Production (in thousand MT)	Percentage to total fruit production	Yield (in kg per hectare)
1987-88	1232.9	43.5	10350.4	37.4	8400
1991-92	1077.6	37.5	8715.6	30.4	8100
1992-93	1136.7	35.5	9223.3	28.0	8100
1993-94	1217.4	38.2	10113.3	27.1	8300
1994-95	1228.3	28.5	10993.3	28.5	9000
1995-96	1283.1	38.2	10810.9	26.0	8400

1996-97	1344.9	37.6	9981.2	24.7	7400
1997-98	1384.9	37.5	10234.2	23.7	7400
1998-99	1401.6	37.6	9781.8	21.4	7000
1999-00	1486.9	37.3	10503.5	23.0	7100
2000-01	1519.0	39.3	10056.8	23.3	6600
2001-02	1575.8	39.3	10020.2	23.3	6400
2002-03	1623.4	42.9	12733.2	28.2	7800
2003-4	1906.7	39.8	11490.0	23.3	6000
2004-05	1970.4	39.7	11829.7	24.0	6000
2005-06	2080.7	39.1	12663.1	22.9	6100
2006-07	2201.4	38.8	13734.0	23.1	6400
2007-08	2201.0	37.6	13997.0	21.3	9400
2008-09	2309.0	37.8	12750.0	18.6	5500
CARG	4.50	-	1.22	-	1.80

Source: Indian Horticulture Data Base. 2009.

Table 4: Important Mango Cultivars in Major Producing Countries

Sl.No.	*Country*	*Cultivars*
1	Australia	Kensington Pride, Banana, Early gold, Glenn, Haden, Irwin,Keitt, Kent, 'Zill'
2.	Bangladesh	'Aswina', 'Fazil', 'Gopal Bhog', 'Himsagar', 'Khirsapati', 'Langra', 'Kishan Bhog', 'Kohinoor', 'Kua Pahari', 'Mohan Bhog',
3.	Brazil	'Bourbon', 'Carlota', 'Coracao', 'Espada', 'Itamaraca', 'Maco', 'Magoada', 'Rosa', 'Tommy Atkins'
4.	China	'Baiyu', 'Guixiang', 'Huangpi', 'Huangyu', 'Macheco', 'Sannian', 'Yuexi No.1'
5.	Costa Rica	'Haden', 'Irwin', 'Keitt', 'Mora', 'Tommy Atkins',
6.	Ecuador	'Haden', 'Keitt', 'Kent', 'Tommy Atkins',
7	Egypt	'Alphonso', 'Bullock's Heart', 'Hindi Be Sennara', 'Langra', 'Mabrouka', 'Pairie', 'Taimour', 'Zebda',
8.	Guatemala	'Haden', 'Kent', 'Tommy Atkins',
9	Haiti	'Francine', 'Madame Francis,'
10.	India	'Alphonso', 'Banganapalli', ' Bombay', 'Bombay

		Green', 'Chausa', 'Dashehari', 'Fazli', 'Fernandian', 'Himsagar', 'Kesar', 'Kishan Bhog', 'Langra','Mallika', 'Mankurad', 'Mulgoa', 'Neelum', 'Pairi', 'Samar Behisht Chausa', 'Suvarnarekha', 'Totapuri', 'Vanrag', 'Zardalu', 'Amrapalli', 'Basngalora', ' Gulabkhas',
11	Indonesia	'Arumanis', 'Dodol', 'Gedong', 'Golek', 'Madu', 'Manalagi', 'Cengkir', 'Wangi'
12.	Israel	'Haden', 'Tommy Atkins', 'Keitt,' 'Maya,' 'Nimrod', 'Kent', 'Palmer',
13.	Kenya	'Boubo', 'Ngowe', 'Batwi',
14.	Malaysia	'Arumanims', 'Kula Selangor2', 'Golek', 'Apple Rumni', 'Malgoa', 'Apple Mango', 'Maha-65', 'Tokboon'
15.	Mali	'Amelie', 'Kent',
16.	Mexico	Haden, Irwain , Kent, Manila, Palmer, Senssein, Tomnny Atkin, Vandyke,
17.	Myanmar	'Aug Din', 'Ma Chit Su', 'Sein Ta Lone', 'Shwe Hin Tha',
18.	Pakistan	'Anwar Ratol', 'Baganapalli', 'Chausa', 'Dashehari', 'Golab khas', 'Langra', 'Siroli', 'Sindhri', 'Suvarnarekha', 'Zafran',
19.	Peru	'Haden', 'Keitt', 'Kent', 'Tommy Atkins',
20	Phillipines	Carabao, Manila Super, Pico, Binoboy, Dudul, Pahutan, Senora,
21.	Singapore	'Apple Mango', 'Arumanis', 'Golek', ' Kaem Yao', 'Mangga Dadol',
22.	South Africa	'Fascell', 'Haden', 'Keitt', ;Kent', 'Sensation', 'Tommy Atkins', 'Zill',
23.	Srilanka	'Karutha', 'Colomban', 'Willard', 'Vellai Colomban', 'Pettiamba', 'Malwana amba', 'Parrot Mango and Peterpasand', 'Dapara', 'Hingurakgoda'
24.	Thailand	'Nam Doc Mai', 'Ngar Charn','Okrong','Rad', 'Choke Anand', ' Kao Keaw', 'Keaw Savouy', 'Pimsenmun',
25.	USA	'Keitt', 'Kent', 'Tommy Atkins',
26	Venezuela	' Haden', 'Keitt', 'Kent', 'Tommy Atkins',
27	Vietnam	'Combodiana'

Source: Horticulture World .net

Table 5: Growth in Area under Mango Cultivation in Major states during 1996-97 to 2008-09

(Area in thousand hectares)

Year	*A.P.*	*U.P.*	*Karn.*	*Bihar*	*Maha.*	*W.Bengal*	*Others*	*India*
1996-97	271.4	256.2	116.5	151.8	65.5	55.7	427.8	1344.9
1997-98	276.2	258.7	123.9	153.2	65.5	55.8	457.6	1384.9
1998-99	252.1	240.5	123.8	154.8	110.0	59.3	461.1	1401.6
1999-00	297.5	243.2	124.1	156.0	147.2	60.0	48.9	1486.9
2000-01	306.2	249.1	134.4	139.1	147.2	62.5	484.1	1522.6
2001-02	341.2	253.0	115.4	139.3	164.4	65.4	506.2	1575.8
2002-03	370.3	247.6	117.4	139.5	181.2	66.4	501.1	1623.4
2003-04	402.2	250.5	116.3	140.0	425.8	67.8	504.1	1906.7
2004-05	391.9	247.0	117.5	140.1	432.7	69.1	563.5	1961.9
2005-06	445.5	265.5	120.5	142.7	434.7	72.2	599.6	2080.7
2006-07	471.4	261.4	129.1	140.8	447.7	78.2	625.3	2153.9
2007-08	483.5	265.9	134.6	142.2	455.8	80.9	626.9	2201.4
2008-09	497.7	271.2	141.3	144.1	457.0	86.0	711.7	2309.0
CARG	6.94	0.49	1.77	-0.42	49.80	4.53	5.56	6.89

Source: National Horticulture Board, Others include Orissa, Tamil Nadu, Kerala, Gujarat, Goa, Madhya Pradesh, Haryana, Punjab etc.

Table 6: Growth in Production of Mango in Major states during 1996-97 to 2008-09

(Production in thousand Kg.)

Year	*A.P.*	*U.P.*	*Karn.*	*Bihar*	*Maha.*	*W.Bengal*	*Others*	*India*
1996-97	56.3	3548.0	1106.5	910.4	196.5	66.8	896.5	9981.0
1997-98	3314.1	1722.3	176.4	1838.9	65.5	547.4	1572.3	10234.2
1998-99	2269.6	2418.7	1176.5	1858.1	196.5	226.5	1635.0	9781.8
1999-00	2379.6	1106.7	1179.9	1871.9	500.5	666.0	2799.0	10503.5
2000-01	2449.5	2250.3	1291.4	1112.5	500.5	380.5	2161.5	10237.0
2001-02	2445.8	1950.4	1130.6	1253.5	559.6	585.0	2095.3	10020.2
2002-03	2932.1	4021.3	1098.2	1255.6	615.9	228.8	2541.7	12733.5

2003-04	3217.2	2100.1	1111.2	1540.1	629.8	405.9	2485.7	11490.0
2004-05	3135.2	2585.6	1105.9	865.5	634.3	460.8	2817.9	11605.2
2005-06	3565.4	2784.5	1303.7	978.5	645.8	492.5	2892.7	12663.1
2006-07	3865.2	2980.5	1368.8	1306.9	646.3	549.8	3016..5	13734.0
2007-08	4157.9	3365.0	1223.3	870.4	710.9	623.2	3026.9	13996.8
2008-09	2522.0	3465.9	1284.4	1329.8	712.8	548.9	2855.6	12749.8
CARG	-2.42	-0.19	1.34	3.84	21.9	4.53	60.14	2.31

Source: National Horticulture Board , Others include Orissa, Tamil Nadu, Kerala, Gujarat, Goa, Madhya Pradesh, Haryana, Punjab etc.

Table 7: Productivity of Mango in Major states during 1996-97 to 2008-09

(Productivity kg per hectare)

Year	*A.P.*	*U.P.*	*Karn.*	*Bihar*	*Maha.*	*W.Bengal*	*Others*	*India*
1996-97	11980	13840	9500	5997	3000	12000	4270	7400
1997-98	12000	6660	9490	12000	1000	9952	3482	7400
1998-99	9000	10050	9500	12000	1793	3320	3547	7000
1999-00	8000	4550	9510	12000	3400	11100	4589	7100
2000-01	8000	9000	9630	7400	3400	6088	4465	6600
2001-02	7170	7700	9800	8900	3400	8944	4141	6400
2002-03	8000	16280	9350	8970	3390	3446	5071	7800
2003-04	8000	8380	9560	11000	1479	5985	4930	6000
2004-05	8000	10460	9400	6180	1466	6511	5005	5900
2005-06	8010	10488	10819	6857	1486	6821	4824	6086
2006-07	8220	11400	10600	9300	1400	7000	4184	6400
2007-08	8600	12706	9100	6100	1600	7700	5167	6400
2008-09	5100	12800	9100	9200	1600	6400	4054	5500
CARG	-10.37	-0.62	0.32	4.10	-16.34	6.73	0.40	-2.56

Source: National Horticulture Board, Others include Orissa, Tamil Nadu, Kerala, Gujarat, Goa, Madhya Pradesh, Haryana, Punjab etc

Table 8: Exports of Mango from India from during 1994-95 to 2008-09s

Year	Quantity in thousand metric ton			Total value in Crore Rs.		
	Mango	Pulp	Total	Mango	Pulp	Total
1994-95	25.4	45.03	70.40	34.46	80.70	115.25
1995-96	22.7	38.51	60.78	36.03	84.61	120.64
1996-97	24.78	44.88	69.66	40.32	105.01	145.33
1997-98	42.89	73.59	116.43	45.87	123.31	169.18
1998-99	45.41	79.13	124.54	38.13	138.56	176.69
1999-00	34.63	71.55	106.18	72.38	196.52	268.90
2000-01	36.43	76.54	112.97	74.35	204.65	279.00
2001-02	44.43	81.00	125.43	76.74	241.34	318.08
2002-03	38.02	84.15	122.21	80.25	286.09	366.34
2003-04	60.55	110.52	171.07	84.94	317.45	402.39
2004-05	58.11	111.93	170.04	88.74	358.21	446.95
2005-06	62.58	135.06	197.64	92.74	402.45	495.19
2006-07	64.15	133.16	197.13	95.84	456.42	552.16
2007-08	68.23	151.65	219.19	99.95	498.99	598.94
2008-09	70.15	177.00	247.15	101.53	526.80	627.81
Increase (%)	176.06	291.11	250.06	194.26	552.27	447.73
CARG	15.13	19.40	16.72	12.95	36.82	29.64

Source: National Horticulture Board, CAGR= Cumulative Annual Growth Rate.

Table 9: Yearwise Area under Mango Cultivation in Selected States and All India during 1996-97—2008-09

(Area in thousand hectares)

Year	A.P.	Maha.	W.Bengal	Total of selected states	Indices (Base 1996-97=100) Selected	All States India
1996-97	271.4	65.5	55.7	392.6	100	100
1997-98	276.2	65.5	55.8	397.5	103	103
1998-99	252.1	110.0	59.3	421.4	107	104

1999-00	297.5	147.2	60.0	504.7	128	105
2000-01	306.2	147.2	62.5	515.9	131	113
2001-02	341.2	164.4	65.4	570.8	145	117
2002-03	370.3	181.2	66.4	617.9	158	120
2003-04	402.2	425.8	67.8	859.8	119	142
2004-05	391.9	432.7	69.1	893.7	128	145
2005-06	445.5	434.7	72.2	952.4	143	155
2006-07	471.4	447.7	78.2	997.3	154	160
2007-08	483.5	455.8	80.9	1020.2	160	163
2008-09	497.7	457.0	86.0	1040.7	165	171
CARG	6.9	49.8	4.5	13.7	13.7	5.9

Source: Indian Horticulture Data base, 2009.

Table: 10 Year-Wise Production of Mango in Selected States and All India During 1996-97 to 2008-09

(Production in thousand MT)

Year	*A.P.*	*Maha.*	*W.Bengal*	*Total of selected states*	*Indices (Base 1996-97=100) Selected States*	*All India*
1996-97	3256.3	196.5	66.8	3519.6	100	100
1997-98	3314.1	65.5	547.4	3927.0	109	102
1998-99	2269.6	196.5	226.5	2692.6	86	98
1999-00	2379.6	500.5	666.0	3546.1	101	105
2000-01	2449.5	500.5	380.5	3330.5	93	103
2001-02	2445.8	559.6	585.0	3590.4	102	100
2002-03	2932.1	615.9	228.8	3767.8	107	128
2003-04	3217.2	629.8	405.9	4252.9	121	115
2004-05	3135.2	634.3	460.8	4230.3	120	116
2005-06	3565.4	645.8	492.5	4703.7	134	126
2006-07	3865.2	646.3	549.8	5061.3	144	138
2007-08	4157.9	710.9	623.2	5492.0	156	140
2008-09	2522.0	712.8	548.9	3783.7	107	128
CARG	-1.87	21.9	60.1	9.0	9.0	10.7

Source: Indian Horticulture Data base 2009.

Table 11: Year Wise Yield of Mango in Selected States During 1996-97 to 2008-09

(Yield kg per hectare)

Year	A.P.	Maha.	W.Bengal	Average yield of selected states	Indices (Base 1996-97=100) Selected States	All India
1996-97	11980	3000	12000	8993	100	100
1997-98	12000	1000	9952	7950	88	100
1998-99	9000	1793	3320	4704	53	95
1999-00	8000	3400	11100	7500	84	96
2000-01	8000	3400	6088	5829	65	89
2001-02	7170	3400	8944	6505	73	86
2002-03	8000	3390	3446	3912	44	105
2003-04	8000	1479	5985	5155	58	81
2004-05	8000	1466	6511	5325	60	80
2005-06	8010	1486	6821	5435	60	98
2006-07	8220	1400	7000	5540	62	86
2007-08	8600	1600	7700	5967	64	86
2008-09	5100	1600	6400	4367	49	74
CARG	-4.8	-3.89	-3.89	-4.3	-4.3	-6.2

Source: Indian Horticulture Data base 2009

Table 12: Area, Production and Yield of Mango in Chittor District of Andhra Pradesh during 1998-99 to 2008-09

Year	Area in thousand hectare	Production in thousand kg	Yield in kg/hectare
1998-99	33.0	106.8	3,236
1999-2000	42.8	342.1	7,772
2000-01	45.1	360.2	7,986
2001-02	45.6	368.9	8,090
2002-03	47.8	382.7	8,006
2003-04	52.7	421.8	8,000
2004-05	48.9	391.3	8,002

2005-06	50.7	396.5	7,822
2006-06	53.4	402.7	7,541
2007-08	56.1	409.6	7,302
208-09	58.9	508.7	8,636
Total	517.0	4091.7	—
Average	47.0	371.2	7, 977
CARG	7.1	39.7	15.2

Source: Directorate of Economics and Statics Government of Andhra Pradesh

Table 13: Area, Production and Yield of Mango in Krishna District of Andhra Pradesh During 1998-99 to 2008-09

Year	*Area in thousand hectare*	*Production in thousand kg*	*Yield in kg/hectare*
1998-99	61.2	803.4	13,127
1999-2000	61.3	490.5	8,000
2000-01	61.4	491.5	8,004
2001-02	65.0	492.7	7,580
2002-03	67.5	539.9	7,999
2003-04	72.5	579.9	7,986
2004-05	62.0	495.5	7,996
2005-06	65.8	530.6	8,063
2006-06	72.6	552.7	7,613
2007-08	75.9	585.6	7,715
208-09	80.4	607.5	7,565
Total	745.6	6169.8	—
Average	67.8	560.1	8,272

Source: Directorate of Economics and Statics Government of Andhra Pradesh

Table 14: Area, Production and Yield of Mango in Chittor and Krishna (Combined) Districts of Andhra Pradesh during 1998-99 to 2008-09

Year	Area in thousand hectare	Production in thousand MT	Yield in kg/hectare
1998-99	94.2	910.2	9,662
1999-2000	104.1	832.6	7.998
2000-01	106.5	851.7	7,997
2001-02	110.6	861.6	7,790
2002-03	115.3	922.4	8,000
2003-04	125.2	1001.7	8,000
2004-05	110.9	887.1	7,999
2005-06	118.5	927.2	7,824
2006-06	126.0	955.4	7,582,
2007-08	132.0	995.2	7,539
208-09	139.3	1116.2	8,011
Total	1332.6	10261.3	-
Average	121.1	932.8	7,710
CARG	4.4	2.1	-1.55

Source: Directorate of Economics and Statics Government of Andhra Pradesh

Table 15: Share of Area and Production of Mango in Chittor and Krishna (Combined) Districts to Total Andhra Pradesh during 1998-99 to 2008-09

(Area in thousand hectare and Production in thousand MT)

Year	Area CD	Area AP	Share #	Production CD	Production AP	Share #
1998-99	94.2	276.2	33.4	910.2	2269.6	40.1
1999-2000	104.1	297.5	35.0	832.6	2379.6	35.0
2000-01	106.5	206.2	34.78	851.7	2449.5	34.8
2001-02	110.6	341.2	32.42	861.6	2445.8	35.2
2002-03	115.3	370.3	31.14	922.4	2932.1	31.2
2003-04	125.2	420.0	31.13	1001.7	3217.2	31.1
2004-05	110.9	391.2	28.30	887.1	3135.2	28.3

2005-06	118.5	445.5		927.2	3565.4	
2006-06	126.0	471.4	28.28	955.4	3865.2	24.7
2007-08	132.0	483.5	26.45	995.2	4157.9	23.9
208-09	139.3	497.7	27.30	1116.2	2522.0	44.3
Total	1332.6	---	------	10261.3	------	------
Average	121.1	------	-------	932.8	------	-------
CARG	4.4	-2.42	------	2.1	-2.42	------

Source: Directorate of Economics and Statics Government of Andhra Pradesh, Note—CD combined districts, AP=Andhra Pradesh, # Share of combined districts to Andhra Pradesh (%).

Table 16: Area, Production and Yield of Mango in Sindhudurg During 1999-00 to 2008-09

(Area in hectare, Production in kg. and Yield kg/ha)

Year	*Area*	*Productive Area*	*Production*	*Yield*
1999-00	20015	11697	52043	4450
2000-01	22020	12298	39355	3200
2001-02	22734	13803	45548	3000
2002-03	23098	14477	49221	3400
2003-04	23267	15847	53879	3400
2004-05	23427	17047	55232	3240
2005-06	23577	18141	59885	3300
2006-07	23707	19397	64688	3335
2007-08	23852	20529	69798	3400
2008-09	23992	21809	74368	3410
CARG in %	1.98	8.64	4.20	-2.34

Source: Directorate of Horticulture, Govt.of Maharashtra

Table 17: Area, Production and Yield of Mango in Aurangabad during 1999-00 to 2008-09

(Area in hectare, Production in MT, Yield kg/ha)

Year	*Area*	*Productive Area*	*Production*	*Yield*
1999-00	13262	2648	7612	2870
2000-01	13810	2965	9364	3200
2001-02	14258	3195	10545	3300

2002-03	14916	3428	11655	3400
2003-04	15109	4336	14741	3400
2004-05	15259	4636	15994	3450
2005-06	15415	4911	16942	3450
2006-07	15574	5211	10856	3465
2007-08	15744	5371	18664	3475
2008-09	15919	5671	19735	3480
CARG in %	2.0	11.42	15.92	2.12

Source: Directorate of Horticulture, Govt.of Maharashtra

Table 18: Area, Production and Yield of Mango in Malda During 1990- 2009

(Area in hectare, Production in kg. and Yield kg/ha)

Year	*Area*	*Production*	*Productivity*
1990	21680	62000	2860
1991	21800	205000	9400
1992	21900	55000	2510
1993	21910	175200	8000
1994	22000	21000	950
1995	22200	260000	11700
1996	22400	22000	980
1997	22420	220000	9810
1998	23200	65000	2820
1999	24080	270000	11210
2000	24150	105000	4350
2001	24259	253876	10450
2002	24500	63678	2600
2003	24550	86000	3500
2004	24850	135000	5430
2005	25250	150000	5940
2006	25500	180000	7060
2007	25900	175000	6760
2008	26300	190000	7220
CARG	0.76	10.86	8.02

Source: District Horticulture Office, Malda

Table 19: Area, Production and Yield of Mango Growing Blocks of Malda in 2009

Block	*Area*	*Share (%)*	*Production -MT*	*Share (%)*	*Yield*
English Bazar	9156	34.68	46335	25.36	5060
Ratua11	2542	09.63	28986	15.34	11403
Ratua 1	2540	09.63	25845	13.68	10175
Manik Chak	3793	14.37	27412	11.59	7226
Old Malda	2122	08.04	21895	14.81	10318
Kalia Chak 11	1892	07.17	15425	11.11	8152
Kalia Chak 1	1596	06.04	7273	05.19	4795
Chanchal	1624	05.84	7673	3.82	4479
Harish Chandra Pur	1135	04.60	7156	3.76	6030
Total	26400	100.00	190200	100.00	7273

Table 20: Area, Production and Yield of Mango Growing Blocks of Murshidabad, in 2009

Block	*Area*	*Share (%)*	*Production MT*	*Share (%)*	*Yield*
1. Lalgola	3085	19.79	22471	17.82	7282
2. Suti-11	3068	19.69	21841	17.32	7119
3. Murshidabad-Jiaaganj	2590	16.62	19745	15.65	7623
4. Farakka	1005	6.49	9191	7.29	915
5. Raghunathganj	934	6.03	8768	6.95	939
6. Belganga-11	850	5.49	8533	6.77	10038
7. Bhagwangola-11	810	5.23	8298	6.58	10244
8. Berhampur	645	4.16	5699	4.52	8836
9. Domkal	552	5.54	4900	3.89	8876
10. Haroharpur	549	3.52	4872	3.86	8874
11. Nouda	482	3.11	4439	3.52	9210
12. Jallanji	412	3.09	3888	3.08	9436
13 Others	505	3.24	3457	2.75	6845
Total	15587	100.00	126102	100.00	7937

Source: District Horticulture Office, Murshidabad

Table 21: Market Arrivals of Mango in Chittor and Krishna Districts in Andhra Pradesh

(Quantity in metric tons and Price in rupees)

Year	*Bangarupallem*		*Chittor*		*Damancheruvu*	
	Quantity	*Price*	*Quantity*	*Price*	*Quantity*	*Price*
1997-98	11307	2500	28721	3000	44426	5000
1998-99	3522	4500	17292	5000	28118	4000
1999-00	10499	3500	58[illegible]19	2000	81825	2000
2000-01	3346	4250	14915	5200	22777	4000
2001-02	33423	2000	57321	3316	31612	3500
2002-03	7004	3000	19872	5536	34700	3000
2003-04	13750	4220	13096	4340	44025	3000
2004-05	31214	5840	27994	7828	46490	2500
2005-06	33491	3533	19975	5100	38307	2500
2006-07	-	-	8732	-	49031	3000

Year	*Putur*		*Tirupati*		*Nunna*	
	Quantity	*Price*	*Quantity*	*Price*	*Quantity*	*Price*
1997-98	18651	3250	9125	2500	-	-
1998-99	7856	4000	2876	5000	20542	5074
1999-00	38903	3000	16710	2700	60000	5077
2000-01	8600	4000	3270	4500	52000	5386
2001-02	13371	3500	13421	2500	62058	5015
2002-03	-		9650	4518	46824	5916
2003-04	-		21411	2966	59285	7000
2004-05	-		19288	4011	27710	6867
2005-06	-		22257	3078	76538	5514
2006-07	-		17794	4380	66720	6163

Source: AMC Offices of respective market Yards, - means Not available, Quantity= quintal and Price= Rs per quintal

Table 22: Monthly Whole Sale Price Index of Mangoes in India (1995-2006)

Year	Base Year 1993-94=100				
	April	May	June	July	Average
1995	175.2	109.7	125.5	105.0	128.9
1996	141.3	119.5	137.3	156.2	138.7
1997	173.8	104.9	111.9	95.4	121.5
1998	191.0	195.8	204.7	242.0	208.4
1999	222.7	118.3	111.0	124.8	144.2
2000	208.6	168.5	180.6	174.6	183.1
2001	181.8	157.9	129.9	146.7	154.1
2002	196.6	163.5	149.8	160.2	167.5
2003	201.4	176.9	197.9	197.9	193.5
2004	240.0	223.4	176.8	176.8	204.3
2005	247.9	240.4	210.9	210.9	227.5
CARG (%)	3.53	8.16	3.52	4.76	6.52

Source: Ministry of Commerce and Industry, Government of India

Table 23: Price Spread for a Ton of Mango in Different Marketing Channels (Value in Rs)

NO	Particulars	Channels				
		I	II	III	IV	V
1	Mango Grower					
	Sale Price	3600 (28.0)	3300 (34.7)	4400 (33.6)	3700 (52.9)	6000 (100.0)
	Marketing Costs	------	------	200 (1.4)	------	-----
	Net Price Received	3600 (28.8)	3300 (34.7)	4200 (32.1)	3700 (52.9)	-------
2	VT/CA/PHC					
	Purchase Price	3600 (28.0)	3300 (34.7)	----	-------	--------
	Marketing Cost	200 (1.6)	300 (3.2)	-----	-------	-------

	Sale Price	4400 (35.2)	4400 (46.3)	-----	--------	-------
	Net Margin/Profit	600 (4.8)	800 (8.4)	----	--------	-------
3	Local Whole seller					
	Purchase Price	4400 (35.2)	4400 (46.3)	4400 (33.6)	3700 (52.9)	----
	Marketing Cost	150 (1.2)	800 (8.4)	150 (1.1)	400 (4.7)	-----
	Sale Price	5100 (40.8)	6300 (66.3)	5300 (40.5)	4900 (67.1)	------
	Net Margin/Profit	550 (4.4)	1100 (11.6)	750 (5.7)	800 (9.4)	------
4.	UCTs/Whole Seller					
	Purchase Price	5100 (40.8)	-------	5300 (40.5)	----	-------
	Marketing Cost	1900 (15.2)	--------	1900 (14.5)	-------	--------
	Sale Price	9100 (72.8)	-------	3900 (71.0)	------	------
	Net Margin/Profit	2100 (16.8)	-------	2100 (16.0)	-------	------
5	Retailer					
	Purchase Price	9100 (72.8)	6300 (66.3)	9300 (71.0)	4900 (67.1)	
	Marketing Cost	1000 (8.0)	850 (8.9)	950 (7.3)	850 (9.7)	
	Sale Price	12500 (100)	9500 (100)	13100 (100)	8400 (100)	
	Net Margin/Profit	2400 (19.2)	2350 (24.7)	2850 (21.4)	2650 (23.5)	
	Gross mark. Margin	8900 (68.0)	6200 (65.3)	8700 (66.4)	4700 (47.1)	
	Consumers Purchase Price	12500 (100)	9500 (100)	13100 (100)	8400 (100)	

Source: Field data. *Note:* Figures in parentheses indicate percentages to consumer's purchase price

Table 24: Price of Mango in Malda during 2004-2006 (per quintal)

Variety	*May*		*June*		*July*	
	Max.	*Min*	*Max*	*Min.*	*Max.*	*Min*
			2004			
Gopalbhog	850	700	1000	900	----	----
Himsagar	----	----	1300	1000	-----	-----
Langra	-----	-----	1200	950	-----	-----
Laxmanbhog	-----	-----	1000	700	-----	-----
Amrapali	-----	-----	1500	1050	1100	950
Fazli	N.A.	N.A.	800	800	1600	1000
Guti(generic variety)	800	650	650	400	800	600
			2005			
Gopalbhog	----	----	600	400	N.A.	N.A.
Himsagar	-----	-----	550	450	N.A.	N.A.
Langra	-----	-----	1100	600	N.A.	N.A.
Laxmanbhog	-----	-----	600	400	N.A.	N.A.
Amrapali			1300	800	N.A.	N.A.
Fazli			900	700	1200	900
Guti(generic variety)			400	250	500	400
			2006			
Gopalbhog	N.A.	N.A.	700	500	N.A.	N.A.
Himsagar	N.A.	N.A.	1200	700	N.A.	N.A.
Langra	N.A.	N.A.	1100	750	N.A.	N.A.
Laxmanbhog	N.A.	N.A.	800	600	N.A.	N.A.
Amrapali	N.A.	N.A.	1300	900	N.A.	N.A.
Fazli	N.A.	N.A.	800	700	1800	900
Guti(generic variety)	N.A.	N.A.	450	350	500	450

Source: Agricultural Marketing Department, Englishbazar, Malda

Table 25: Cost and Returns of Different Varieties of Mango in Malda, West Bengal

Variety	*Prodn./Tree(Qtl)*	*No. of Tree /ha*	*Prodn.(Qtl/ha)*	*FGP(Rs/Qtl)*
1.Aswina	8	15	120	725
2.Fazli	9	18	162	725
3.Langra4	7	05	35	890
4. Himsagar	6	05	30	725
5. Laxmanbhog	5	02	10	600

6.Gopalbhog	5	05	25	550
Total	-	50	38	-

Continued the Annexure

Variety	*Cost of Operation/tree*	*Total Cost of Operation(Rs/ha)*	*Revenue (Rs/ha)*	*Net Income (Rs/ha)*
1. Aswina	600	9,000	87,000	78,000
2.Fazli	600	10,800	1,17,140	1,06,340
3.Langra	600	3,000	31,150	28,150
4. Himsagar	600	3,000	21,750,	18,750
5. Laxmanbhog	600	1,200	26,000	4,800
6.Gopalbhog	600	3,000	13,750,	10,750
Total	-	30,000	2,76,790	2,46,790

Source:-Field data, FGP(Rs/Qtl)= Farm gate Price

Table 26: Cash Flow Statement of Alphanso Mango

Year	*Cap.Cost*	*Main.Cost*	*Mark.Cost*	*Total Cost*	*Tot.Income*	*Net Income*
1	79,408	0	0	79,408	0	-79,408
2	36,748	0	0	36,748	0	- 36,748
3	34,676	0	0	34,676	0	-34,676
4	19,228	0	0	19,228	0	-19,228
5	14,936	0	0	14,936	0	-14,936
6	0	25,104	18,180	43,284	54,992	11,708
7	0	25,104	22,220	47,324	67,213	19,889
8	0	25,104	26,260	51,364	79,434	28,070
9	0	25,104	31,310	65,414	94,709	38,295
10	0	35,146	43,430	78,576	1, 31,371	52,795
11	0	35,146	46,460	81,606	1, 40,536	58,930
12	0	35,146	52,520	87,666	1, 58,867	71,201
13	0	35,146	58,580	93,726	1, 77,198	83,472
14	0	35,146	66,660	1, 01,806	2, 01,639	99,833
15--30	0	62,760	81,115	1, 43,875	2, 44,411	1, 00,536

Source: Field data,

Table 27: Cash Flow Statement of Kesar Mango in Aurangabad

Year	Cap.Cost	Main.Cost	Mark.Cost	Total Cost	Tot.Income	Net Income
1	44,649	0	0	44,649	0	-44,649
2	18,118	0	0	1,81,18	0	-18,118
3	21,004	0	0	21,004	0	-21,004
4	24,615	0	0	24,615	0	-24,615
5	27,859	0	0	27,859	0	-27,857
6	0	21,029	8,380	29,359	28,254	-1,105
7	0	21,029	11,901	32,930	40,363	7,433
8	0	21,029	17851	38,880	60,545	21,665
9	0	21,029	26,181	47,210	88,779	41,589
10	0	21,029	35,702	56,731	1, 21,089	64,358
11	0	36,800	47,602	84,402	1, 61,452	77,050
12	0	36,800	57,123	93,923	1, 93,743	99,820
13	0	36,800	65,453	1, 02,253	2, 21,997	1,119,744
14	0	36,800	71,403	1, 08,203	2, 42,179	1, 33,976
15-30	0	52,572	76,164	1,28,736	2, 58,324	1, 29,588

Source: Field data

Appendix 1: Model Scheme of Mango

Mango *(Mangifera indica)* is the leading fruit crop of India and considered to be the king of fruits. Besides delicious taste, excellent flavour and attractive fragrance, it is rich in vitamin A&C. The tree is hardy in nature and requires comparatively low maintenance costs.

Mango occupies 22% of the total under fruits comprising of 1.2 million hectares, with a total production of 11 million tons. Uttar Pradesh and Andhra Pradesh are having the largest area under mango each with around 25% of the total area followed by Bihar, Karnataka, Kerala and Tamil Nadu.

Mango fruit is utilised at all stages of its development both in its immature and mature state. Raw fruits are used for making chutney, pickles and juices. The ripe fruits besides being used for desert are also utilised for preparing several products like squashes, syrups, nectars, jams and jellies. The mango kernel also contains 8-10 percent good quality fat which can be used for soap and also as a substitute for cola in confectionery.

Fresh mangoes and mango pulp are the important items of agri-exports from India. India's main export destinations for mango are UAE, Kuwait and other Middle East countries with a limited quantity being shipped to European market. Although, India is the largest mango producing country, accounting about 60% of world production, the export of fresh fruit is limited to Alphonso and Dashehari varieties. India's share in the world mango market is about 15 percent. Mango accounts for 40 percent of the total fruit exports from the country. There is good scope for increasing the area and productivity of mango in the country.

Climate:

Mango can be grown under both tropical and sub-tropical climate from sea level to 1400 m altitude, provided there is no high humidity, rain or frost during the flowering period. Places with good rainfall and dry summer are ideal for mango cultivation. It is better to avoid areas with winds and cyclones which may cause flower and fruit shedding and breaking of branches.

Soil:

Mango comes up on a wide range of soils from alluvial to laterite provided they are deep (minimum 6') and well drained. It prefers slightly acidic soils (pH 5.5 to 7.5)

Varieties:

Though there are nearly 1000 varieties of mango in India, only following varieties are grown in different states : Alphonso, Bangalora, Banganpalli, Bombai, Bombay Green, Dashehari, Fazli, Fernandin, Himsagar, Kesar, Kishen Bhog,Langra, Mankhurd, Mulgoa, Neelam, Samarbehist, Chausa, Suvarnarekha, Vanaraj and Zardalu.

Recently some mango hybrids have been released for cultivation by different institutes / universities. A brief introduction to such varieties is presented below:

Mallika - It is a cross between Neelam and Dashehari. Fruits are medium sized cadmium colored with good quality, reported to be a regular bearer.

Amrapali - It is a cross between Dashehari and Neelam. It is a dwarf vigorous type with regular and late bearing variety. It yields on an average 16 t/ha and about 1600 plants can be accommodated in one hectare.

Mangeera : It is a cross between Rumani and Neelam. It is a semi vigorous type with a regular bearing habit. Fruits are medium sized with light yellow colored skin, firm and fiberless flesh and sweet to taste.

Ratna : It is a cross between Neelam and Alphonso. It is a regular bearer and free from spongy tissue. Fruits are medium sized with excellent quality. Flesh is firm and fiberless, deep orange in color with high TSS (19-21 Brix).

Arka Aruna : It is a hybrid between Banganapalli and Alphonso with regular bearing habit and dwarf in stature. About 400 plants can be accommodated per hectare. Fruits are large sized (500-700 gm) with attractive skin color. Pulp is fiberless, sweet to taste (20-22 Brix). Pulp percentage is 73 and the fruits are free from spongy tissue.

Arka Puneet : It is a regular and prolific bearing hybrid of the cross between Alphonso and the Banganapalli. Fruits are medium sized (220-250 gm) with attractive skin color, having red blush. Pulp is free from fiber, pulp percentage being 70 percent. Fruits are sweet to taste (20-22 Brix) with good keeping quality and free from spongy tissue. It is a good variety for processing also.

Arka Anmol : It is a semi-vigorous plant type from the cross between Alphonso and Janardhan Pasand. It is also a regular bearing and free from spongy tissues. Fruits ripen to uniform yellow color. Keeping quality of the fruit is very good and it is suitable for export. It has got excellent sugar and acid blend and fruits weigh on an average about 300 g Pulp is orange in color.

Propagation:

Farmers should always get vegetatively propagated, true to type plants from recognised nurseries. Inarching, veneer grafting, side grafting and epicotyl grafting are the popular methods of propagation in mango.

Planting: Land should be prepared by deep ploughing followed by harrowing and levelling with a gentle slope for good drainage. Spacing varies from 10 m x 10 m, in the dry zones where growth is less, to 12 m x 12 m, in heavy rainfall areas and rich soils where abundant vegetative growth occurs. New dwarf hybrids like Amrapali can be planted at closer spacing. Pits are filled with original soil mixed with 20-25 kg well rotten FYM, 2.5 kg single super phosphate and 1 kg muriate of potash.

One year old healthy, straight growing grafts from reliable sources can be planted at the center of pits along with the ball of the earth intact during rainy season in such a way that the roots are not expanded and the graft union is above the ground level. Plants should be irrigated immediately after planting. In the initial one or two years, it is advisable to provide some shade to the young plants and also stake to make them grow straight.

Training and pruning:

About one meter from the base on the main trunk should be kept free from branching and the main stem can be allowed thereafter spaced at 20-25 cm apart in such a way that they grow in different directions. Branches which cross over/rub each other may be removed at pencil thickness.

Fertilizer Application:

In general, 170 gm urea, 110 gm single super phosphate and 115 gm muriate of potash per plant per year of the age from first to tenth year and thereafter 1.7 kg, 1.1 kg, and 1.15 kg respectively of these fertilisers per plant per year can be applied in two equal split doses (June-July and October). Foliar spray of 3% urea is recommended before flowering in sandy areas.

Irrigation:

Young plants are watered frequently for proper estalbishment. In case of grown up trees, irrigation at 10 to 15 days interval from fruit set to maturity is beneficial for improving yield. However, irrigation is not recommended for 2-3 months prior to flowering as it is likely to promote vegetative growth at the expense of flowering.

Inter Cropping:

Inter crops such as vegetables, legumes, short duration and dwarf fruit crops like papaya, guava, peach, plum, etc. depending on the agro-climatic factors of the region can be grown. The water and nutrient requirements of the inter crops must be met separately.

Plant Protection:

Mango is prone to damages by a large number of pests, diseases and disorders. The recommended control measures for most important and common among them are briefed below :

Mango hopper: Two sprays (at panicles emergency and at pea size of fruits) of carbaryl (0.15%), monocrotophos (0.04%) or phosphamidan (0.05).

Mealy bug : Ploughing inter spaces in November and dusting 2% methyl parathion @200 g per tree near the trunk and fixing 20 cm wide 400 gauge polythene strips around the trunk with grease applied on the lower edge in January as prophylactic measures and two sprays of monocrotophos (0.04%) at 15 days interval as control are needed.

Powdery mildew: Two to three sprays of wettable sulphur (0.2%) or Kerathane (0.1%) at 10-15 days interval.

Anthracrose : Two sprays of Baristin (0.1%) at fortnight interval.

Malformation: One spray of 200 ppm NAA in October followed by deblossoming at bud burst stage in December - January.

Fruit drop: Regular irrigation during fruit development,

timely and effective control of pests and diseases and spraying 20 ppm NAA at pea size of fruits.

Harvesting and Yield:

Graft plants start bearing at the age of 3 - 4 years (10-20 fruits) to give optimum crop from 10-15th year which continues to increase upto the age of 40 years under good management.

Post Harvest Management:

Storage: Shelf life of mangoes being short (2 to 3 weeks) they are cooled as soon as possible to storage temperatue of 13 degree Celcius. A few varieties can withstand storage temperature of 10 degree Celcius. Steps involved in post harvest handling include preparation, grading, washing, drying, waxing, packing, pre-cooling, palletisation and transportation.

Packaging: Mangoes are generally packed in corrugated fiber board boxes 40 cm x 30 cm x 20cm in size. Fruits are packed in single layer 8 to 20 fruits per carton. The boxes should have sufficient number of air holes (about 8% of the surface area) to allow good ventillation.

Financial institutions have also formulated mango financing schemes in potential areas for expansion of area under mango. Individual mango development schemes with farm infrastructure facilities like well, pumpset, fencing and drip irrigation system etc. have also been considered.

Farm model for financing one hectare mango orchard is furnished in the Annexure I.

Unit Cost: The unit cost varies from state to state. The cost presented here is indicative only. The entrepreneurs and the bankers are requested to consult our Regional Offices for the latest information in this regard. The unit cost estimated for this model scheme is Rs.34400/- per ha capitalized up to the fifth year. The break-up details are given in Annexure I.

Financial Analysis : Results of financial analysis are indicated below :

NPW at 15% DF : Rs 39058 (+) , BCR at 15% DF : 2.34 , IRR : 25.59%

Detailed analysis is presented in Annexure II.

Margin Money : The margin money assumed in this model scheme is 5% of the total financial outlay.

Interest Rate : Interest rate may be decided by the banks as per the guidelines of RBI.

Security : Banks may charge such security as permissible under RBI guidelines.

Repayment : The bank loan with interest is repayable within 14 years with 7 years grace period as shown in Annexure-III.

Annexure - I: Cost and Income from Mango Cultivation (Rs. per ha) --Spacing : 10m x 10m, Plant Population : 100

Estimated cost:

Sr. No.	*Particulars*	*Year*					*Total*
		1	*2*	*3*	*4*	*5*	
1	Planting material	2200	--	--	--	--	2200
2	Manures & Fertilisers	3000	1100	1100	1400	1400	8000
3	Plant protection	1100	600	600	700	700	3700
4	Sprayer & implements	1500	--	--	--	--	1500
5	Fencing	2500	--	--	--	--	2500
6	Irrigation	1800	500	500	500	500	3800
7	Labor	3200	1200	1200	1500	1500	8600
8	Intercropping	1500	--	--	--	--	1500
9	Miscellaneous	600	500	500	500	500	2600
	Total	17400	3900	3900	4600	4600	34400

Projected income:

	Year										
	1-5	*6*	*7*	*8*	*9*	*10*	*11*	*12*	*13*	*14*	*15th onwards*
Yield (q/ha)	0	25	35	50	60	70	80	90	100	110	120
Gross value @ Rs. 4.50 / kg	0	11250	15750	22500	27000	31500	3600	40500	45000	49500	54000
Maintenance (Rs/ha)	0	4600	6000	6000	6200	6200	6200	6200	6200	6200	6200
Net Income (Rs/ha)	0	6650	9750	16500	20800	25300	29800	34300	38300	43300	47800

Annexure - II: Financial Analysis (Mango Cultivation)

Particulars/Year	*1*	*2*	*3*	*4*	*5*	*6*	*7*	*8*	*9*	*10*	*11*	*12*	*13*	*14*	*15-25*	
Capital cost(Rs.)	17400	3900	3900	4600	4600											
Maintenance cost (Rs.)	0	0	0	0	0	4600	6000	6000	6200	6200	6200	6200	6200	6200	6200	
Total cost(Rs.)	17400	3900	3900	4600	4600	4600	6000	6000	6200	6200	6200	6200	6200	6200	6200	
Income(Rs.)	0	0	0			11250	15750	22500	27000	31500	36000	40500	45000	49500	54000	
Net Benefit(Rs.)	-17400	-3900	-3900	-4600	-4600	6650	9750	16500	20800	25300	29800	34300	38800	43300	47800	
DF at 15%	0.870	0.756	0.658	0.572	0.497	0.432	0.376	0.327	0.284	0.247	0.215	0.187	0.163	0.141	0.738	
PWC at 15% df	15130	2949	2564	2630	2287	1989	2256	1961	1762	1533	1333	1159	1008	876	4576	44012
PWB at 15% df	-15130	-2949	-2564	-2630	-2287	2875	3665	5394	5913	6254	6405	6411	6306	6120	35276	59058
NPW at 15% df	15046															
BCR	1.34															
IRR	25.59%															

Annexure III: Repayment Schedule (Mango Cultivation)

Total Financial Outlay(Rs) 34400, Margin money @ 5% of TFO((Rs.) 1720, Bank Loan(Rs.) 32680

(Amount in Rs.)

Year	*Loan disbursed*	*Net benefit*	*Interest @ 12%*	*Deferred Interest*	*Payment of Interest*	*Payment of Interest*	*Repayment Principal*	*Total repayment*	*Net Surplus*	*Principal Outstanding*
1	16530	-17400	0	1984	0	0	0	0	-17400	16530
2	3705	-3900	445	2428	0	0	0	0	-3900	20235
3	3705	-3900	445	2873	0	0	0	0	-3900	23940
4	4370	-4600	524	3397	0	0	0	0	-4600	28310
5	4370	-4600	524	3922	0	0	0	0	-4600	32680
6		6650	3922		3922	0	0	3922	2728	32680
7		9750	3922		3922	0	0	3922	5828	32680
8		16500	3922		3922	0	2500	6422	10078	30180
9		20800	3622		3622	650	2500	6772	14028	27680
10		25300	3322		3322	650	4000	7972	17328	23680
11		29800	2842		2842	650	5000	8492	21308	18680
12		34300	2242		2242	650	5500	8392	25908	13180
13		38800	1582		1582	650	7000	9232	29568	6180
14		43300	742		742	672	6180	7594	35706	0

Repayment period is 14 years including 7 years grace